200 Letters,

62 Years,

and a War

By Antoinette and Domenic Lombardi

Edited by Maryanne Christiano-Mistretta

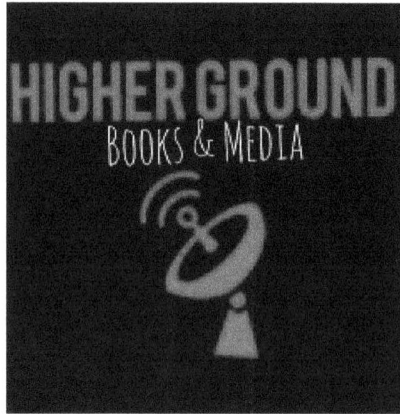

Higher Ground Books & Media
Springfield, Ohio.
http://www.highergroundbooksandmedia.com

Printed in the United States of America 2019

200 Letters, 62 Years, and a War

By Antoinette and Domenic Lombardi

Edited by Maryanne Christiano-Mistretta

Domenic's Dedication

This book is being dedicated to my wife—the one person who gave me the courage to survive the bitter cold Korean winters, the blistering hot summers and some moments of total despair. Without her support I might not have been able to survive those months in Korea, and more than likely wouldn't be here today to write these memoirs.

I must say, with all my heart, thanks to my wife, Toni Lombardi

Antoinette's Dedication

I'd like to dedicate this book to Domenic—my true love who married me and gave me the happiest life. I don't know what I would do without him. I, too, love him with all my heart. Thank you, Domenic

Foreword

By Domenic

The story you are about to read is true, as I have lived and experienced it during my basic training to the actual days I was in Korea. My only regret is that time has erased most of the memories of events that took place while in Korea. To the best of my knowledge, everything you will read is factual.

Why was Korea labeled as the "Forgotten War"? Look back to the end of World War II. The USA and our allies defeated the Nazi War Machine, and in the Pacific brought the Japanese to their knees in defeat. We, as a nation, at this time were victorious and the people back home were lad that the war was over. Then it became obvious that we were heading toward another confrontation in the Far East, a tiny peninsula called Korea.

President Truman committed our troops to Korea, and we were in a new type of war that they called a "police action." The people back in the States were never concerned about such a small obscure country thousands of miles from the USA.

No one thought it important enough to get involved. Whoever heard of this Korea anyway? The only thing I knew about Korea was what I had read or seen in our history books.

It is difficult to explain to people that the Korean Conflict wasn't a "police action," but a real honest to goodness war. One has to look at the list of the wounded, killed and missing in action names to fully realize that this was not a "police action."

To the returning Korea veteran of a very unpopular war, and a war that wasn't victorious, our nation did not know how to react. Consequently, the returning Korea veteran never received any recognition from the American public.

Never did a Korean veteran complain about his treatment when he returned to civilian life. Most of us were proud that we served our country and if we had to do it again, we certainly would.

Why, you may ask, would we do it again after the way we were greeted? The answer is very simple. With all our faults in government, this is by far the only place on earth that I would like to live on. To the men that were there— no explanation is needed.

The good old USA is the best on the planet. Believe me.

Chapter 1

By Antoinette

I was born Antoinette Pavone on June 1, 1929. I was raised in West Orange, New Jersey. We didn't have any money, we rented. My mother had four children, two boys, two girls; I was the baby of the family. My father worked in Thomas Edison in West Orange. My father was a strict man from Italy, coming to the United States at the age of 18 and served in World War I.

During those times we played with the neighbors in our street, games like 1-2-3 Red Light and Take a Giant Step. Nothing really too exciting, except that at the age of 7, one day I saw a man who threw away a cigarette butt. I picked it up and smoked it. After a beating from a father, he asked me if I'd ever do that again.

I said I wouldn't. And I kept my word. Those days were strict, and even though my father was a firm man I loved him with all my heart. He was definitely my hero for what he did, fighting for our country; and for what he did for our family. He was a good man who once carried me on his shoulders everywhere after I hurt my ankle.

My mother was a gem. In my husband's words, she was a "gem" and "an angel." Though I think my father was jealous of the attention she gave us, as he tried to keep us away from her. After dinner, my siblings and I would sit at the table, discussing school and other topics, but my father kept speaking to my Mom in Italian, alienating us.

I definitely missed my mother's attention. I felt something was missing in my life. I wanted to get close to my mother, but I couldn't. She never told us how she felt. My father was always there. My husband refers to him as a "Gestapo."

Even though I was a tomboy, my biggest dream was to fall in love and get married. That's just what they did in those days.

In high school I joined a lot of clubs with my girlfriends: camera clubs, science clubs and gym, which was my favorite. It was a close little clique. Rosemary, who lived down the street from me, was a girl I hung out with. As teenagers we met boys together. This was during World War II. I've experienced air raids and food rations. It was a scary time, but being a teenager, going out with friends made life a little more secure.

When I was 16, I met a nice guy at a dance. His name was Jimmy. Sometimes he'd come to my house and my father said, "Get rid of him." There was nothing wrong with Jimmy. He had a lovely mother and came from a good home. My father was so severe in his beliefs I would have got hung from a tree if I got pregnant. Every time I went out, my father was on my mind. So, I dated in fear…definitely.

Breaking up with Jimmy wasn't a big deal even though I liked him, as I had plenty of other boyfriends. Back in those days you could play the field and it was okay Another guy I was dating was named Joe. He was a great guy too. My father actually liked him and I was surprised. Joe was generous. He took me to see the Statue of Liberty and to St. Patrick's Cathedral. We enjoyed walking around Rockefeller Center and looking at the tree at Christmas time. We did everything, but I had to be home at 10 p.m. I always obeyed, of course, as I would panic about what my father would do if I was late.

Eventually I broke up with Joe, because I met someone else I really liked—Domenic Lombardi.

Chapter 2

By Domenic

I was born in 1928 at the Orange Memorial Hospital, in Orange, New Jersey.

I lived on Jefferson Street, right across the street from Becker's Dairy. Milk, in those days, was delivered by horse and wagon. I used to sit on the front steps to watch as the horse and wagons lined up along the curb waiting to go in and have the horse and wagon stored for the night. Jefferson Street, at the time, was lined with cobble stones and not paved as we know today's roads. That was my entertainment as a little boy.

We used to play a game called Red Line, marbles, and played basketball. As a teenager, we'd go to dances in a gymnasium in a girl's settlement house. A volunteer would play records.

Antoinette "Toni" and I met at a very early age, around 13-years-old—at the State Movie theatre. Yeah, 10 cents got us into the State Movie if we could get a dime from our parents.

I used to dance with Antoinette's older sister, Connie. She was much older than me; a refined person, a beautiful woman, very well mannered, too nice, to tell you the truth. One night she introduced me to Antoinette, and I wanted to date her because she was in my age bracket. She was chubby, more to love. Oh my God! She was jolly and easy to get along with. She wasn't a sour puss. She liked to have fun. She was a personality. I had a lot to choose from and I chose her. Girls would come in my front door and I'd sneak out the back.

Antoinette left notes on my car. I threw them away. I always cared for Antoinette, but I had other interests. Though she was my main target.

I was going out with a girl named Zella and she dumped me after I was fooling around with Antoinette. I wasn't too good to go out with; I was wild. I didn't care about going out with girls. I went out with my buddies.

Most of our teen years were spent in the Settlement House and Miss Robs, a place we used as a dance hall. From there it was a trip to the lake.

Toni and I parted until after high school. Soon after we reconnected, I was drafted and found myself in Korea—June 13, 1951. Toni was my lifeline to home with her letters. She wrote at least one per day.

After 62 years of marriage, five children, and 13 wonderful grandkids, I have to consider myself to be the luckiest guy in the world. And if I had to do it all over again, I wouldn't change a thing.

Chapter 3

By Antoinette

Domenic Lombardi was a handsome Italian boy, with dark hair and green eyes. Domenic and I met at the Settlement House dance. Originally Domenic asked my sister to dance. But she was disinterested and pushed him over to me. So, he asked me, and I said, "Yes."

At the time Domenic was going out with another girl named Zella. She worked at a Five and Ten in Orange. One day I went shopping there and Zella told me, "All he talks about is *you*." I didn't want to be second fiddle, so I broke off with Domenic. Soon after that Zella broke up with Domenic.

I had both Domenic and Joe calling me at the same time. I picked Domenic.

When we got back together, he said he loved me and wanted to go steady. So, we did, and I was soon known as "Domenic's girlfriend." Guys knew to stay away. Domenic was a little jealous, but not overbearing like my father was. In fact, he was nothing like my father, which was refreshing.

I had to sneak out and see Domenic. The jealousy my father once had towards my mother, turned to me. He didn't want anyone to take his place in my life. It was terrible sneaking around, though we had a great time going to the movies and dancing. Larry's Pizzeria was one of our favorite places we'd frequent after the dances. Shopping on Main Street in Orange was also a favorite thing to do.

We'd also visit Domenic's family—but not mine. And I learned from that, I always told my kids, "No sneaking, I want to meet who you're going out with."

What made Domenic different from other teenage boys, at the time, was he had a car—an apple green Mercury convertible. The color was so green you could see the car for miles! Every time it rained, the roof leaked, and I'd get wet. He couldn't afford a new roof, but it was nice on a sunny day when the roof was down.

I graduated high school in 1948. Domenic had dropped out three months prior to graduation. He was supposed to graduate in 1947, but instead got a job at Nevins Church Press, a printing plant. He did various jobs during his time there.

Domenic and I dated a couple years. By the time we were 18, legal adults, we realized we were truly in love with each other and decided to make plans for a future. I was getting tired of going home and him going back to his house. It was stupid and I suggested getting engaged. At the time Domenic was drafted to fight in the Korean War. He said he wanted to get engaged but I'd have to wait until he got back on leave. Originally, he was registered for the draft for World War II, but was never called. This time, he wasn't so lucky.

Before Domenic went to service, his mother threw him a party at their house with family and friends. My family came to the party too. At this time, I let them know we were serious. My father showed no emotion.

Before he left, he gave me a Victrola and records to go with it. They included: "The Tennessee Waltz," by Patti Page; "Time Out for Tears," by Nat King Cole; "Jezebel," by Frankie Laine; "I Won't Cry Anymore," by Tony Bennett; and four by Eddie Fisher: "Any Time," "Trust in Me," "I Can't Go On Without You," and "Talk of the Town."

We felt bad that he was going to service and every Sunday we went to see him in Fort Dix, where he had basic training.

During his seven-day furlough we were able to see each other. We did fun things like visit Budd Lake, see fireworks, and go down the Jersey shore. I was so quiet during our rides Dom used to kid me and ask if I was mad. Then I'd just smile and sit closer to him. I was a shy girl. When Dom brought me to his home, it was hard for me to get acquainted with his family. I wasn't sure if they liked me or not, so I'd sit quietly in the parlor, alone, and never went where the group gathered. Sometimes I'd walk out of the house to avoid company. This got Domenic mad. He wanted me to be more sociable so everyone would like me. I only ate a little too. I was chubby, but I lost the weight by eating normal. I didn't eat much in front of Domenic.

Domenic later shared, in a letter from Korea, how mixed up he was during his time in Fort Dix, knowing that the end result would be going to war. He stayed strong, trying to mislead everyone so they wouldn't worry or feel sorry for him.

After the seven-day furlough, Domenic was shipped out by train to San Francisco, California, and then left by boat to Japan.

I didn't really feel left behind because I was busy working as a secretary for Monroe Calculating in Orange. On weekends, I'd go to stay with Domenic's family, as if he was still there with them. That brought comfort to me and helped ease my loneliness. I'd also hang around with the girls and go bowling. It would kill the time as I awaited letters from Domenic. He looked forward to the letters too. He said, "All servicemen look forward to letters. That's their link to home."

In the first letter he wrote to me, he said, "We should have got married." His letters always ended with "love," "your boyfriend Dom," and "Don't forget to wait!" But one time he wrote, "Don't wait; I don't think I'm coming back." He was up in the front lines.

Chapter 4

By Domenic

January 21, 1951 – Fort Dix, New Jersey.

Life could never be more miserable than the first night in the army camp. Mine was and I was no different from the many there that night. I had no idea what was to be expected of us from one minute to the next. It seemed like endless hours of shots and miles of needless walking from one barrack to the other for whatever reason I cannot recall today.

Some could not make the transition and simply passed out from sheer exhaustion before the night was finished.

I can't remember what we ate, but all I know is that I was so hungry it could have been laced with poison.

Basic training started as soon as we got assigned to our barracks. Luck would have it we were put near the ranges at the far end of Fort Dix. January is a cold month and being out on a windswept desert made it a lot colder. Yes, we had our service club across the road from our barracks. How many times do you think we even had a chance to go in it?

Life in basic starts early in the morning and ends late afternoon. We attend classroom lectures that simply stretch one's limitations for snoozing, only to be whacked over the head by the cadre when caught—and many were.

What did we know when we were asked to serve our country? Nothing. But for sure we were going to learn very fast as we found out in the ensuing days ahead. We crammed every piece of army weaponry into our days while in class, sitting on that cold asphalt. Then came the actual using of each piece of equipment on the ranges.

Days flew by as we continued our training. Nights were semi-free, only after you cleaned your rifle and equipment—a must before anyone in that barracks could go to sleep. All rifles must be inspected by the cadre and passed by him and then locked in the rifle rack. Then—and only then—are the men in the barracks allowed to go to sleep; no exceptions.

Letter writing and snacking was possible up to 10 p.m.; then it was "lights out" in the barracks. They did have one room set aside for letter writing after "lights out," but very few had any energy after the long day we had just finished—and what was to come up in the morning.

Life in a barracks full of all different kinds of characters could make for an interesting day, as I recall. First there are the neat and tidy, then comes the lazy ones who just don't care—nothing in between. Reverie in the morning was a battle with each trying to gain access to a sink to shave. Once you win one battle, the next is to get into the shower. Soap and water is flying everywhere as you approach. Once you find a stream of water, you are in a position to shower. All this has to be done in time for our morning inspection of the troops.

Although the barracks looked like we just had World War II, it was a matter of minutes and everything was back in shape for our inspection.

Chapter 5

By Domenic

As the weeks passed, the days got longer, and the nights got shorter. Marching out to the ranges to fire our weapons and marching back really gave you little time to clean up before you were able to plot down in bed. On some of our easier days, we did have a change of pace.

After eight weeks passed, we finished our first half of basic. We were now going to take eight weeks of advanced training. Our barracks were World War II vintage—used by the soldiers.

Every Friday we had a G.I. party. That's when all the men got to scrub their floors and clean around their banks. Of course, when you poured too much water on the floor it leaked through to the floor below. The guys would yell up and we tried to be more careful.

This one wise kid downstairs thought he was some kind of boss. He always came to the bottom of our stairs and yelled up orders for us to stop dripping water down on the guys below. We got tired of this joker and decided to teach him a lesson the next time we had our G.I. party.

The day arrived and we filled our trash can with water and carried the can over to the head of the stairs. We just knew that this kid had to come and show his authority. When he came to the bottom of the stairs and yelled up, we were waiting. We threw the water at him. He went right to the cadres and squealed on us. Corporal Bright came upstairs and demanded to know, "Who threw the water?"

Of course, no one answered him. So, he made all the guys upstairs carry their packs and rifles down to the parade grounds. We marched up and down the parade grounds, making plenty of noise. The men sleeping in the other barracks were yelling for us to be quiet. After an hour, we went back into our bunks.

Corporal Bright and I never saw eye-to-eye. I didn't like him, and I knew he didn't care about me. Every time we marched out to the ranges, he would be walking alongside the men and would whack them with a swagger stick as we marched along. I would watch him as he drifted back to where I was and I would say to him, "You had better not hit me with that stick."

He didn't like what I said but he didn't hit me either. But he got back at me in other ways. He would always try to give me a detail when he saw me going to the orderly room for my pass to go home. I always told him, "If we go overseas together and we are in combat, don't get in front of my rifle."

Chapter 6

By Domenic

The remaining weeks were coming to a close for our company, which meant we would graduate and receive our new assignments. The night of the graduating party I don't think there was anyone sober. When the party ended and we returned to the barracks, nothing in the barracks was recognizable. Bunks that were double-deckers were now stacked three high. Bedding was strewn all over the place. Mattresses were out on the barracks' roofs. The place looked like a total mess. To this day I can't recall where we all managed to bed down for the night.

The following day we received orders for our next assignment. We would get our 30-day furlough and report back to Fort Dix for the start of our next assignment overseas to the Far East Command. That meant we were most likely going to Korea.

The 30-day furlough went by pretty fast. I knew that I was going to Korea, but never gave it much thought because our nation called it Police Action. I never thought of it as a war.

The day arrived and I had to leave for Fort Dix to catch my train. Pete and Bruno Manna drove me to the bus in East Orange. I said my good-byes to everyone and made a hasty move for the door. As I walked out the door, I saw my father burst into tears. I ran out to the car and we drove off. All the buses were waiting for us at the American Legion Hall on South Munn Avenue in East Orange.

I said "Good-bye" to Pete and Bruno as we boarded the busses. We pulled into Dix and there was a troop train waiting. Most of the guys boarding the train had their families there to wish them a safe journey. Then, after what seemed like hours, the train started to move out of the siding. People cheered and cried as we left them behind on the platform. This would be the first time I had ever been away from home, knowing that I would not be returning for some time to come. I wasn't feeling too happy at this time, being on a troop train. I had heard many stories from ex-G.I.s that a ride on a troop train is not very exciting and could be a hassle.

It was early noon as we departed. The train was heading west, and our final destination would be Camp Stoneman, California. Each group or passenger car had a packet commander or officer in charge of that particular car. We picked our seats and sat watching as the train wound its way out of the state. We also had railroad conductors on board to assist us on our journey. Being a troop train, it would not make stops except for supplies or military personal along the way.

After a while we settled down and enjoyed the scenery. Between each seat was a table that gave us plenty of room to play cards or read or whatever. I was beginning to wonder how we would be getting our chow on this train. We were told that each car would be called to eat. We had no idea how this would take place. I heard many stories from veterans that eating aboard a troop train was no easy task. Carrying your mess kit and coffee cup while trying to navigate the train (as it swayed back and forth) was miserable, to say the least.

The moment of truth had arrived as we were called to chow. We followed our packet commander through a couple of cars and into a real dining car with tables and waiters to take orders. Well, this certainly wasn't what we had expected rom the army! It was a real treat for us to sit down and get our food served to us. I could see that this part of our trip would be enjoyable. That was my first surprise on the train.

Surprise number two came when we were ready for bed that night. We were on Pullmans (sleeping cars) and our conductor changed our seats into two very comfortable beds with a curtain for privacy. Well, this really made our first day aboard this troop train a complete success. We settled in for the night and to my amazement, I really got a sound sleep rolling along the tracks. The next morning our conductor remade all our beds back to seats while we were in the dining car eating our breakfast.

Along the route, the train did stop a few times and when it did a lot of the guys jumped off and headed for the beer halls. It got so bad that for the rest of our journey the military police were at the train station and no one was allowed off the train.

It was early evening and we were approaching the Donner Pass. It was strange that we were in warmer climate when we began the climb and when we got near the top, there was about two feet of snow. They had to hook a large steam engine to our train to help push our train up and over the pass. It wasn't long that we were down on the valley floor and it was warm again. We went from cold to sweltering heat of the desert.

Our fourth day found us pulling into Camp Stoneman. After four days aboard that train we were glad to get off. We got temporary sleeping quarters. We didn't receive any blankets or pillows to sleep with.

I never knew that San Francisco, which was warm during the days, got very cold at night. During the day we were all dressed up in our summer Class-A uniforms. That night it was so cold I slept with my uniform on. I even covered myself with the mattress and slept on the springs.

The next day we had to wait for a ship, so I got called for kitchen police. It was the biggest mess hall I had ever seen. I was told that it could feed 5000 men. There must have been a lot of truth to that because I cracked case after case of eggs and tossed them into a giant mix master as tall as I am. I must have cracked thousands of eggs that morning for breakfast.

Although no one likes to get put on kitchen police, how would I have gotten the experience of seeing firsthand what a monumental job it was to feed our men? Of course, I wouldn't ask or volunteer for kitchen police.

Chapter 7

By Domenic

While in Camp Stoneman we were getting anxious waiting for our ship. Three days later it arrived, and we were told to move out—bag and baggage. With our packs, duffle bags and our rifles, we moved down to meet the busses. The busses brought us down to a ferry boat, the Yerba Buena, which took us across the harbor to where our ship was docked. The dock was crowded with well wishers seeing their loved ones off; an Army band with a singer; and the Red Cross passing out orange juice and donuts.

We were ordered to board and there was a steady stream of green moving up the gang plant and disappearing inside the ship. When I got my assigned bunk, I dropped my gear down and headed back up on deck.

I watched as the people on the dock were waving to their loved ones up on deck. The band struck up Bali Hi as the tugs moved us away from the dock. We could still hear the band as we moved up the harbor.

I was amazed at the size of the Golden Gate Bridge as we passed under it. No one left the railing as we watched the coast of California slowly disappear over the horizon.

Little did we expect what was going to happen next, as we were told that the water out of the Golden Gate could be very rough and it sure lived up to its reputation. The ship began to pop up and down like a cork as we headed out to sea. Many started heaving into garbage cans.

I decided to go to the very back of the ship and found myself a private spot. I must have sat there for hours. When I returned to my bunk, what a mistake; the stench from the men heaving was too much to bear. I had to go back up on deck for some air. I never went back down until the next morning.

I saw my buddy Lumley lying in his bunk. He really looked green in color and couldn't move. I asked him, "Do you want me to get you something to eat?"

"No…no," he said. "Just bring me an orange if you can."

I went for breakfast and to my surprise there were not many takers that morning. The next surprise was that we had tables and chairs in our mess hall. I knew that I must eat, for I had survived the worst part of the journey and food might be the answer to keep from getting seasick. I was really satisfied that I was able to eat such a big breakfast and hold it down.

Chapter 8

By Domenic

A woman named Kate Holliday was on our ship. She was a writer and authored the book, "Troop Ship." She roamed among the troops and spoke to most of us. She also signed autographs. Everyone was anxious to meet her. Kate Holliday was some person—a very sociable, nice lady. That was some job being around 4500 guys or more, being the only lady. Some were wise guys, making not so nice comments. She took a big responsibility; she was right out there with the guys. I'm assuming she was in her late 20s or early 30s.

Holliday rounded up guys to put on a talent show. She fit right in with the guys. Most of them treated her with upmost respect.

One of the first days at sea we had a storm. It was scary. I thought, *we didn't get there yet and we're all gonna drown.* I stood near the lifeboats in case something happened. That Pacific Ocean can be nasty. Most of the time on the ship, the weather was stormy, and the ship bounced around like a cork.

We had plenty of good chow. A typical breakfast at sea would be eggs, coffee, corned beef hash, cereal, and prunes. Dinner could be turkey with dressing, cranberries, coffee, bread, potatoes, and apple salad. You could get all you want to eat.

The ship had plenty of shower rooms and wash basins. You never had to wait.

You meet all different people from all over the United States, all going to the same place. I hoped the war was over before we reached Japan. Wishing thinking…that would never happen.

Each day I was further from Antoinette. I missed her terribly. All I saw was water and couldn't wait to see land.

We traveled across the International Date Line and lost a day. We were getting irritated being cooped up.

Finally, we docked in Yokohama, Japan, 11 a.m. on a Sunday. But we stayed on the boat until 3 p.m. When the gangplank finally went down and we were ready to get off the ship, directly in front of us was a huge sign above a warehouse on the dock. It read: "Through this port passes the finest soldiers in the world."

"Move out!" came our orders and we all picked up our baggage and went down the gangplank to the waiting trains—which were nothing but old converted milk cars with wooden bunks lining each side of the car. We were told that we would be going through some tunnels on our way. We didn't give it much thought until we entered that first one. We were being pulled by a steam locomotive and the smoke from the tunnel. We found out very quickly that if you wanted to breathe you better get down close to the floor of the car where the smoke thinned out. We passed through at least three more tunnels on our way to Sasebo, Japan.

From the boast, we boarded troop trains and took a three-hour ride. Looking out the window, the first thing I noticed was how unusually short the Japanese were. They moved in a hurry. The homes they lived in made me feel sorry for them. They were all close together; one-room sheds no bigger than a garage. Streets were no bigger than a driveway, with no cars. They probably couldn't afford them anyway. I only saw American cars. Roads weren't paved. Farmers worked by hand, as there wasn't farm equipment.

When we got off the train, children ran to the train to get gum and cigarettes from the G.I.s. Women wore wooden shoes and baggy pants. Most wore kimonos and you couldn't tell if they were 16 or 60. They all looked alike and dressed alike. Young people didn't have their own style at the time.

Next we got on another train to Camp Drake in Sasebo, Japan. This old Japanese camp had all the accommodations needed. I was really surprised to see how well this camp was maintained. The barracks were huge and could hold a company of men. They had all the stores and recreation facilities right in the barracks compound. The one thing that caught my fancy was that we defeated the Japanese and here we were in one of their camps being protected by Japanese guards.

We waited for our ship to come in, for our journey to Korea.

Chapter 9

By Domenic

I don't remember how many days we waited, but the ship finally arrived. We were bussed down to the dock to our waiting ship. There it stood—a huge black vessel with the name "Maru" painted across the bow. It looked like a converted cruise ship, not a military vessel. We went on board and walked into a huge room, like a ballroom, stripped of all its furnishings. We picked a spot on the floor that would be our sleeping quarters for our journey. There we dropped our gear.

A captain spoke to us over the P.A. system: "This ship isn't equipped with any radar. Nor does it have any weapons to defend itself." He gave us the exact location of all the life jackets and wished us a safe journey.

After hearing that this ship was an easy target for the enemy, I decided to stay up on the dock right under the life jackets.

The following morning it was hazy, but we could see the coastline of Korea. Our ship docked in Pusan. It was evident that there was a war going on by all the military personnel and equipment moving around this area. We were bussed to the 8069 Repo-Depot, a camp for replacements and returning veterans.

Breakfast was our first meal in Korea. During the meal the First Sergeant gave a briefing on what to expect after we leave the Repo-Depot. He assigned us to our outfits and advised us to take a hike around the mountains surrounding the city of Pusan.

Climbing the mountain was a beautiful sight looking down on the city of Pusan. As we walked along the ridge line, I saw large mounds of dirt neatly in rows, surrounded by a stone wall of bricks, forming some sort of a boundary. I asked a young Korean soldier what those mounds were.

"Graves of my people," he said. "We have a custom of burying our dead, high on the mountain, looking down on the city or village below. The more important the person; the higher up he is buried."

We continued our hike across a small Korean Village, perched halfway up on the side of the mountain. When we finally made our way down the mountain to the Repot-Depot we were assigned to our new outfits and the next thing we did was to board trains—similar to the type of trains in Japan. We traveled a short distance and then went on foot to our new outfits. We caught up to Company B just as they had come off a patrol and were making camp for the night. We were then interviewed by the Company Commander.

"What kind of training have you had?"

I told him, "Light, heavy weapons."

He assigned me to the 57 recoilless rifle squads. That happened to be the only weapon that I never saw or had any training on in basic.

I was introduced to the squad leader who offered me to bed down in his pup tent for the night. I didn't have a partner yet to share our shelter half to make a pup tent. It was now dark—and I mean dark! I had no idea where I was or what to expect.

It seemed like I had just fallen asleep when someone was pulling on my legs to get me up. It was still dark out. I got up and got myself a new squad. I was told we were going on a search and destroy mission.

Oh great, I thought. *I haven't even seen the country and here I am going out in the dark of night.* I was given six rounds of 57-ammo to carry in a pouch slung over my head, with three products in the front and three in the back. I also carried my M1 rifle and our packs. Trucks came and I thought, *Great, we won't have to walk.* Well, the trucks did carry us to the bottom of this mountain. Then we got off.

It was still dark out and we started our climb up this mountain. Once on the top of the mountain, we walked for what seemed like miles. I sure didn't expect to walk all this distance without coming in contact with the enemy. Soon it was getting light out. I was completely in awe when I saw the Korean countryside in the light of morning. We were on top of the mountain and we could see for miles—nothing but mountains. We had walked so far that my feet developed blisters. We must have walked for about two hours and our first contact was with one of our own Rangers who was dug in up this mountain. Coming down the trail toward us was a medic team carrying a G.I. When he passed right by me, I saw my first casualty of war. I suddenly realized that this could be me or any of our men next.

We went through the rangers' lines and a couple hundred yards down we came upon an enemy bunker. We quickly set up our mortars and got our 57s in a position to fire on that bunker. I loaded the round into the 57 and tapped Ricard, a fellow G.I., on his helmet. This meant that the round was in and he could fire the weapon. Ricard put that round right in the window of that bunker!

We fired another round and it also went right in through the window. We fired a third round and it hit the top of the bunker window. I said to myself, *No way could anyone survive that*. As I was thinking of all we had done, we started to get return fire from that bunker. Then all hell broke loose as the gooks* zeroed in on us with their mortars. Believe me, I couldn't get any closer to that ground, praying that none hit near me.

*[*Editors note: "Gooks" is a derogatory term used by soldiers in war to refer to the enemy in Korea. Domenic Lombardi has not used this term since and has Korean friends. It was his choice to keep the term in the book to illustrate the sign of the times.]*

It seemed like hours as the rounds kept coming in and exploding all around us as we lay there. It finally stopped and we were told to move back to a safer area. Ricard and Sorrell, my squad leader, told me not to carry those rounds back. They told me to bury them right there on the hill.

And who was I to question these veterans? I buried them and then we took off for a safer area. We were then told that we were done with that bunker and had to get back to our trucks. Believe me, the walk back seemed like nothing compared to when we marched out there that morning. We got back to the truck and riding with my new buddies felt as if I've known them my entire life.

Riding on the backs for those trucks would soon become our outfit's way of moving from place to place around Korea. It was my first look at the destruction a war could bring to a nation. How small cities we passed through were totally destroyed with most—or all—buildings leveled to the ground. In some of the larger cities some iron or steel of the buildings remained standing as a monument to the destruction.

We rode, for what seemed like hours, over dirty, dusty roads through village after village. We were never told of our next assignment until the moment we arrived. I was truly fascinated with the ride, viewing the countryside.

Late afternoon, our convoy reached our destination. We camped at the base of this mountain and that night we were to go up and main some of the positions on the hill. It was now dark, and we started our climb up. I had no idea where we'd be going or what to expect. I knew I would not sleep that night while up on that hill.

We moved into our bunkers and we remained alert all night, looking out from our positions. We found out from our squad leader that we were up there to plug a gap in our lines, should the ROK soldiers decide to bug out. I found out that this was a common practice for the ROKs during the beginning of the war. Right in front of our positions stood the ROK soldiers. You could see the gooks shelling their positions.

Our job for the day was done and we moved down off the hill and boarded our trucks again. The next area we ended up in was an area that was to be used in the event an armistice was ever agreed upon. We were assigned to building bunkers for the Kansas Line. Every day we dug positions and built fortifications. We must have filled thousands of sandbags and chopped down numerous trees for the roofs of our bunkers. Our next task was to string barbwire in front of our positions. This was hard, for the ground was mostly solid rock. And we had some trouble driving in our stakes which would hold the barbwire. In some parts of the line it was so steep we had difficulty in stringing the barbwire. After a couple weeks that part of our job was completed.

Again, we boarded our trucks and were off to a new area.

Chapter 10

By Domenic

A month had gone by and it seemed like I was in Korea for years. I was constantly on the move. The road through our small camp was washed out from the heavy rains. We kept rebuilding the road with rocks to hold back the dirt from the running water. Eating our chow was another challenge, trying to keep the rain from our mess kits as we ate. Before you finished your meal, you were sure to have your mess kit water mixed with your food. The only protection we had from the rain was our pup tents. Naturally we didn't stay inside the tents during the day—rain or shine. We got drenched to the skin as we carried out our daily task.

What could be the worst thing you could do while lying in your pup tent while it was raining? I learned by experience that as soaked as the roof of your pup tent looked, it didn't drip down on you. But put your finger up and just touch the roof of your pup tent and you would now get a steady stream of water dripping down on you and you can't stop it no how.

The next thing we learned about keeping dry was to climb into our sleeping bags—wet clothes and all. The heat from your body did an excellent job of drying your clothes. In fact, this was the only way to do so during periods of non-stop rain.

One day while in Camp Burnett, a black kid named Gillian started to act as if he was going crazy and pulled out his 45 pistol. He told us, "I'm going to shoot the platoon sergeant."

We quickly took his weapon away from him and subdued him. At the time, the sergeant didn't realize why we had him down on the ground.

Gillian insisted he was crazy in efforts to get out of front-line duty. It didn't work. He went to the aid station and was informed there wasn't a thing wrong with him.

The weather was not favorable as we made plans for our next assignment. We loaded onto our trucks as it rained. We moved down the road until we came to a river. The bridges in Korea were all destroyed, and our convoy would have to cross the river. With the steady downpour the rivers became swollen and moved rather swiftly. Knowing this, our engineers had a bulldozer on the opposite shore, with a cable stretched across to our side.

The convoy lined up with the larger trucks leading the way and the smaller vehicles in between the larger ones. I believe the width of the river was about the length of a football field.

Our first truck entered the water and the journey across the river began. It was a slow process as we entered the water and were pulled across. The trucks used their own power to help the convoy across. The cable was to keep the convoy moving should one or more vehicles' motor stall in the water.

The water got much deeper as we got closer to the middle of the stream, as it was up over the wheels of our truck. The water moved at a swift rate of speed and the wheels of the truck started to sway as the water crashed up against the side of the truck. I thought that any minute we were all going for a swim in that river. The constant rain kept the water rising and I was thankful when our convoy made it safely to the other side.

This time we were to go up a mountain in front of us. We climbed up a hill in a steady light drizzle. Once on top of the hill, we decided to take a smoke break. About five of my buddies were sitting on logs. Our morale was low—so I decided to liven things up. I secretly took one of my hand grenades, unscrewed the top and emptied the powder.

I put the top back on and walked towards my buddies, making sure they saw what I had in my hand. I pulled the pin and threw the grenade in the middle of the group. They all jumped for their lives! Yet the grenade did nothing but make a little "pop."

I laughed so hard when I saw the looks on their faces. They thought, at first, that I had gone bonkers. Once they recovered from the initial shock, they wanted to kill me. I can say, truthfully, that after that incident our men were fully alert and our morale had improved.

Chapter 11

By Domenic

We never knew where we would be at any time. We just moved from one area to another as we were needed. At night, we'd strain our eyes to see if we could see anyone moving out in front of our bunker. If you ever knew what quiet was, one night on guard up on these mountains, quiet becomes ever so quiet it's scary. You can almost hear your heartbeat as you take a sigh of relief to break the silence.

We moved to rest areas to regroup and check our equipment. Anything that was missing had to be replaced. This meant that we were going up on line or an assault.

For our next assignment, our whole company moved out in the early morning and followed a half road and pathway heading north. We were in a huge valley with mountains to our right. It wasn't long before the gooks spotted our company and started to shell us with mortars. Lucky they were not on target as we took cover. We moved out again when the shelling stopped and we continued up the valley.

As we neared our objective the rounds were coming in more frequent. We moved down the riverbank and used it as our cover as we moved on ahead. Our rifle squads got their orders to move out and assault the hill that lay directly to the right of where we were. They had to cross a clearing before they reached the bottom of the hill they were to assault. By now you could hear all the rifle fire and grenades exploding as our guys made their way up the slope. The gooks were trying to knock out a quad-50 that was right above us on the opposite side of the river from where we were. It came pretty close as one round landed in the river where we were showering.

Then we were ordered to assault the hill. We moved out over the bank and into the valley. We were out in the open now and we headed for the bottom of our objective. As we moved up the slope, rounds and rifle fire came at us from all directions.

Russ, who was a new replacement, was alongside me and Sergeant Henry Lewis. Russ yelled and I turned to see what happened. He called to me, "I'm hit!" and he fell to the ground.

We had to get to our objective so I could not stop to help him. That had to be left to the medics who were with us. It's inevitable that will happen and hopefully not to you.

It seemed like hours for us to get to the top of this hill, but we finally got to the ridge and jumped into a trench that ringed the ridge line. No sooner we jumped into that trench, I looked up to my left and our machine gunner was firing at gooks. I don't think it was seconds later I saw him get shot in the head as he slumped over his weapon. We were just about to get out of the trench when we felt this terrific explosion. I was lying flat down on my face when this round hit and lifted my entire body straight up to the top of the trench. Each time it hit I did the same no matter how hard I tried to hold on to the ground beneath me.

I believe that we received at least four rounds in our immediate area. Was I relieved when it stopped!

We reported to our platoon leader and he informed us that those rounds were from our own 75 recoilless rifles. They were supposed to be hitting to the right of our positions and someone made an error. I am not sure if those rounds inflicted any wounds or killed any of our guys that day.

I am sure of one thing, and this is if there were any of our guys up near where they were exploding, I am certain that someone got killed or wounded.

Minutes seemed like hours as we waited our next move. Then we were called forward to try and knock out this enemy bunker that was keeping our rifle squads from advancing up to the next ridge line.

Sergeant Henry Lewis lay there in the trench and I said to him, "Come on, they are asking for a fifty-seven forward." I thought, at first, he was wounded for he wasn't moving at all. I yelled to him, "Come on, Sergeant! They are waiting for us!"

Well, he did wake up and we moved up in a position to fire at the gooks' bunker. I fired the first round and it went right into the window of the bunker. I fired another round and it also went into the bunker window. I thought to myself, *How can anyone survive those explosions?*

We moved back and the riflemen tried, once again, to assault that bunker. As we watched them attack the bunker, all we could see was a wall of hand grenades coming out off the bunker window. And our guys had to retreat.

I couldn't believe that there were still men in that bunker after all those rounds. Sergeant Henry Lewis and I moved back to our own position. We were going to dig in for the night. Frank and I, with Gillian, took a position on the side of the hill facing the gooks. Darkness fell and we were receiving our replacements. Because of where the foxhole was, we had to put Frank at the top part because that was the deeper part and I took the lower part. We put Gillian in the middle, between us. Every time a flare went up, Frank and I would look over the side to see if any gooks were sneaking up on our foxhole. Gillian would always try to hold us from looking out, for he said that we were giving away our position.

I told him, "Shut up, for the gooks already know these positions for a couple hours ago they were in them."

The night went by without any attacks from the gooks. I really felt sorry for the new replacements as they dribbled in during the night. I was thinking to myself, *These poor guys, some of them may never see the light of day.*

All night long our 60mm mortars sent up flares to keep the gooks from staging any attacks on our positions. If you ever wondered how long a night is, try surviving one night on a battle line when you never know what to expect next. Thank God the gooks had enough and they, too, must have dug in for the night.

Morning came and for breakfast, Frank and I decided to have some C-Ration, a dry packaged food we had in stock. We didn't have gourmet meals on the hills, and you ate when you got a chance.

As we ate, we saw a black object heading towards us and we dove for cover. Fortunately, the round fell harmlessly down the side of the mountain, below us.

"They must want some of these lousy C-Rations," Frank said.

Later that morning, as our rifle squads battled the gooks to move them from that bunker, Warren McConnell and I moved up in a position where we had a clear field of fire for our 57 recoilless rifle. We sat in a foxhole with our 57 recoilless rifle between us, resting on the edge of the foxhole. We could hear our men trying to take that over a gook bunker from all the rifle fire we heard. Though where we were situated, it was so quiet you could hear the gooks talking across the way.

Then we heard a "pinging" sound. We had no idea what it was. We looked to see if there were any gooks sneaking up. Then I looked over at Warren. "Hey! Warren, your ear is bleeding." Sure enough, he felt his ear and the blood. We had no idea how his car started to bleed. Then we looked at our 57 recoilless rifle and were shocked to see a hole, right through one side of the muzzle. That is how Warren's ear was hit.

There had to be a sniper trying to hit one of us sitting in that foxhole. Thank God the 57 recoilless rifle's barrel was sticking out over the foxhole. It caught the ullet that was probably meant for one of our heads. We thanked God that the 57 was between us that time.

Warren never received first aid from a medic, so it never got recorded as a wound inflicted in combat. We did have our 57 taken away and replaced with a new one. Then some idiot had the nerve to steal our site. We found another foxhole nearby and it was another night of small arms fire with the gooks until early morning.

Our people who worked in the kitchen, in charge of feeding the troops came up on our hill with cases of C-

Rations stacked 10 high. "Wow!" I said, "They expect to be up here for some time."

I don't remember if it was two or three days that we kept our positions. All I remember is one day we were all ordered to pull back off the hill. It seemed that gooks had launched a major counter attack and we had to pull our forces back down into the valley. Well, after we finally got off that hill, I believed that the gooks saw all those cases of food and that is what they were really interested in.

My recollection, as we were moving down off the hill, was of one of our rifle platoon lieutenants standing up firing a B.A.R. (Browning Automatic Rifle) at the gooks, covering us as we moved off the hill. I hate to think of how many of us would not have made it to the bottom without him covering our guys moving down off the hill. I can't even remember if he made it down himself.

Once down the hill, we made our way across the river to the valley floor. We found a huge foxhole and jumped in. Because of all the rain, the hole had about six inches of water in it.

That night we had to dig our new positions. It was a long night as we waited for the gooks to come down and attack.

When morning came, the rain stopped. We looked over at the hill we were on the day before. We could see the 31st Infantry Regiment attacking that hill. We watched as they moved up and pushed the gooks off. Like I said before, those gooks didn't care about that hill as much as they cared for our C-Rations.

With that hill secured, we packed up our gear and off we went to another area.

Chapter 12

By Domenic

Traveling the roads in Korea had to be an experience in itself. The roads were all dirt; at least the ones I traveled on anyway. And crossing over some of those mountain passes would make your hair stand on end. They were high, steep, and dangerous. Any time you travel in a convoy, you're covered from head to toe with dust. As the convoy speeds along, the dust could choke you if you do not cover your face. The only time you could actually look at the scenery was during the monsoon weather and the cold months.

One thing we learned about the people in Korea is that they knew exactly when a convoy was going through their village. All the kids waited along the road as we passed, waiting for the G.I. to throw candy or cigarettes to them. Knowing this, we saved most of our candy and cigarettes to throw to the people along the roads of the villages we passed through.

It was now September 1951. We rode for quite some time to another area we thought would be a rest area. We were told that we were relieving another outfit. Little did we know what to expect as we climbed this hill. The day was hazy and rather warm for the time of year. The trail up was rocky and steep in some areas. What we saw ahead as we climbed seemed to be a treeless mountaintop, dotted with trenches and many bunkers.

At the top we could see that we were out on a finger with the gooks looking at us from three-side. Tracey, my gunner, and I decided to sit atop one of the bunkers to eat our C-Ration. Most everyone was just looking for their positions at this time. We no more than had our C-Ration cans open when all hell broke loose. The gooks must have waited for us to get up there and then when they saw us, out of our bunkers, they blasted us with mortars.

Tracey and I dove for the nearest bunker only to find it was filled to the door. We had no choice at this time to look for another, so we huddled in as close as we could in the doorway. The rounds were coming in rather fierce and plenty. It wasn't long after we got a direct hit on the roof of our bunker.

The concussion was so great that it sent stones, as well as dust, flying in all directions. Tracey, who was right alongside of me, had gotten a concussion from the explosion. Then he yelled, "I'm blind from the concussion." He started to panic and wanted to get up and run. I held him down; for it would have been certain death for him had he left this hole and exposed himself to the mortars that were still coming in at this time.

It seemed like hours that we were under attack. Then as quick as it started, it ended with an unbelievable chilling silence.

"Is everyone okay? I asked my mates in the bunker.

Thank God I got a "Yes."

"How are you doing, Tracey?"

"I could see again."

Next was the job of seeking out our wounded and killed. We ran from trench to trench helping those that could be helped. Some never had a chance and were killed instantly. Many were wounded and treated, and it was now the job of the medics to get these guys down off the hill to the aid station.

We often used Korean work force to help us carry our wounded off the hills. Joe Hoffmann, I, and two others carried our buddy Jack down to the aid station. We took turns going down the steep rocky slopes, carrying the stretcher.

Just as we started to make our way down, I saw two Korean workmen trying to throw a dead G.I. poncho case over the side of the hill. When someone is so mutilated, they are in pieces, this is not a nice thing.

I walked over to them with my 45-pistol pointing at their heads. I said, "If you try that one more time I will shoot." Our guys were supposed to be carried off the hill and buried properly with respect.

As we continued our way down, two black guys were carrying the stretcher with Jack on it. They weren't more than 50 feet and they stopped. They both agreed they were tired.

This went on for a few miles. Joe and I were getting mad because Jack's blood dripped through the canvas stretcher. "When are we getting to the aid station?" Jack asked repeatedly.

All I could say was, "It's just around the next turn, Jack." I can't remember how many times I lied to Jack, for I had no idea how far we had to go. What else could I say to this guy who was bleeding to death right before my eyes?

Joe and I knew that if we continued with these black guys, Jack wouldn't get to the aid station at all. "Let's hoist Jack up over our heads and we could jog the rest of the way," Joe suggested. And we did just that, leaving the other two behind as we jogged down the hill with Jack.

We made it to a waiting jeep. We placed Jack on board and wished him luck. Then away went the jeep with Jack.

It was getting dark and we never were in this area long enough to know the trail back. Somehow, we managed to get back up and moved into our bunkers—all on the alert for a gook attack.

Nothing happened that night and soon it was morning. We got a better view of what we were in for as we looked out towards the gooks' positions. We were out on a finger and we were exposed to the gooks on three sides. Everyone had to keep a low profile while moving about the hill. Most all stayed in their bunkers as this would not provoke the gooks to shower us with their mortars. Although we did keep to our bunkers the gooks never missed a day when they peppered our hill with mortars.

We were lucky to have Big Jim, our cook. He would always try to get a hot meal up to us for breakfast. It wasn't always a successful venture, especially when the gooks found out and in came the mortars.

This one day, just as we were served breakfast the gooks started to shell us. The rounds came so close to the kitchen personnel they just dumped all the food and took off down the hill. To get breakfast, we had to make as few moves as possible, as to not reveal to the gooks what we were doing.

That meant each man was responsible to get out of his bunker and get his own chow. We knew it was a chance you had to take, but that was the only way.

I would go along each bunker and tell the men, "If you want your breakfast, get out now and make it quick!"

Gillian would make his buddy get out so he could bring him some breakfast. One day I caught him and told him, "If you want your breakfast, you have to get out and take the same chances that we all do." I don't think it was fair that he used one of his buddies to get his chow, so he wasn't in any danger. I figured that when he gets hungry, he will come out and he did. A few days passed and then I saw him going to the chow line.

On this particular hill we had strong sturdy bunkers that were easily accessible with a trench alongside. This was a hill where we could see the gooks as well as they could see us. So, most of our days and nights were spent right there in our trenches and bunkers. Watching the gooks.

Sitting up on these hills would try our nerves to a breaking point. Any minute or second a round could come in and if you are out of your bunker and that round happened to land close to you, well, that is all she wrote.

Even with the protection of our bunkers, there was no guarantee that a round could find its way into the trench where we were sitting. That also would be the end for anyone sitting in the trench. We always had an ample supply of hand grenades and ammo. Plus, the weapons and ammo we confiscated from the gooks when the hill was taken from them. We had a pile of gook grenades and an assortment of the gook Burp-Guns in our trench. The gook Burp-Gun was feared by most not because of its deadly fire power but for its weird sound as it fired.

Because we were confined to our bunkers, we had plenty of time to talk and most of the time we played cards. This is where I learned to play Pinochle.

I believe a few weeks passed and, as usual, we struck up a card game when we came off guard. We always sat in the same area when we played cards. We had a trench outside our bunker, and it led into a room-like area in the rear. I can't remember how many of us were sitting at the time playing cards. We usually formed a circle and were really cramped. We had played numerous games before in this same spot, but this time as one of the guys slammed his cards down, we heard a noise that wasn't supposed to be made when you hit a dirt floor.

We all stopped and looked at each other. Our first thought was a land mine set by the gooks when they were kicked off the hill. I got my bayonet and probed around the metal object. I had cleared most of the dirt covering this metal object. It looked to me like it was a huge cover from one of the gook's cooking pots.

I then pried around the edge to lift this cover up. And, sure enough, it was a pot cover. As I lifted the cover to throw it away, I looked down and there was a huge room filled with dead gooks. The one closest to the top of the heap was fully clothed but his face was burned beyond recognition. The smell was so bad I had to close the hold immediately. After covering the hole, we put some extra dirt on top.

I couldn't believe my eyes! Here we were almost a month and right below us was this huge gook underground cemetery. I had often wondered where their dead were when we pushed them off a hill. I never realized that the gooks could dig these huge rooms beneath their positions to push all their dead so we would not find one dead gook when we took over a hill.

We never reported that we had found this underground cemetery because at the time we were more concerned with the live ones out in front of our positions.

I had often wondered if the North Korean government ever went back to retrieve those dead soldiers.

Chapter 13

By Domenic

I guess it was around the end of October 1951, when we were relived from that hill. I wasn't one bit sorry to go. It was like solitary confinement, which gave us little time to move about and clean our equipment or our clothes. That hill would forever remain in my memory. We lost many buddies on that God forsaken hill, including Jack, who we carried down to the jeep. He never made it.

The day before Jack got killed, he received a package from his home in Hawaii. He made me try dried fish and I have him a piece of my pepperoni. We kidded around about our different foods. Jack would always make me smile and say, "It's good, it's good."

I don't remember how Jack and I became friends expect that David, who also came from Hawaii, introduced us. Every year at our Memorial Day parade, I choke up, remembering the day Joe Hoffman, and myself, carried Jack off Finger Ridge.

The weather was still rather warm for this time of year and we drove overland to our new positions. This new area was rather unique, for we were to protect this huge valley with our troops on both sides of us in the mountains. A road wound through our positions and right below the road was a river flowing through our camp. Our mortars positioned our weapons behind the first hill and our 57s were up on a high point of the hill. We had five or six tanks with us in this area. We were protected from the gooks to the north by this finger that ran down to the valley floor. We were not visible from the north if we stayed behind this finger.

I had my lookout hutch up on the side of this finger and I could see the gooks' positions from this hutch. It was our job to pull guard every day at dusk until dawn out on the valley floor. We had outpost out in the valley where our men would go and pull guard. We also had the tanks that would move out into the valley with us and take positions along the valley floor. This was done every day while we were in this valley.

We were shielded from the gooks' view from the back side of this hill. We could spot them a long time before they got close to our positions. I had my forward observers' hutch on the front side of our hill, pretty well hidden from the eyes of the gooks. From this position I would observe any gook's movement in the valley, or anyone coming up the road. Our 60mm mortars were all set on specific targets out in the valley. And when we saw any troop movement, we would fire our mortars. This usually sent them back to their holes and we could almost, without fail, expect a return fire from the gooks.

This was, more or less, our daily routine while in the valley. Nights were a little different. Every night, just as the sun set, we would send out our men to pull outpost guard in the valley. We usually rotated our men so that each group would have equal time out on guard. The tanks attached to the seventh would also set up guard out in the valley with our men.

Things were going smoothly. Each night our guys would hike out to their positions. One night, as our men got halfway out to their positions, the gooks rained down on them a barrage of mortars.

Tracey, who was on guard that night, must have recalled the day he was with me and our bunker was hit with a mortar round. So, when the rounds started to come in, Tracey just went out of his mind and started screaming and crying. He was quickly taken away by our medic and set to our field hospital. I didn't know whatever became of Tracey, for that was the last time I saw him.

Coming back early in the morning, usually we'd find a hot breakfast waiting for us.

I prepared my gear, as I was to be on guard duty in the valley that night. Most of the rifleman's positions were well out in front of the tanks. I was with Mosley, a big black kid. We took up our position off the road about 50 yards in front of a tank. It was a good spot for protection for we had this huge rock we were behind. Guards were rotated, one hour on and one hour off. Although there were others on guard, out there we could not see each other, and we used our sound-powered telephones for communication.

Each hour we would have a position check from our command post. Each position would have his own "identification call word." Around 3 a.m. I was leaning on the rock, straining my eyes, looking down the road. Thank God for hearing, for I heard something long before I could see anything.

Noise was coming down the road toward us. It happened so fast that I never had a chance to wake up Mosely. I knew someone or something was coming down the road. I yelled, "Halt!"

I had not seen anything, but I knew men were walking at a fast pace. It seemed to me that they were not going to stop, so I jumped out onto the road and raised my M1. Once again, I yelled, "Halt!"

I guess they saw I was about to shoot, and they quickly raised their hands above their heads and surrendered. There were five gooks and only the last one was carrying a rifle. The tankers heard all the commotion and I could hear bolt on their 50-caliber click.

"Don't fire!" I yelled. "We got everything under control."

Mosley woke up and couldn't believe his eyes when he saw five gooks standing there with their arms over their heads. We got our helmet and as I kept my rifle on them, we made them empty their pockets and put everything into the helmet. We collected many rounds of ammo for that one rifle and plenty of hand grenades—so many that we filled two steel pots.

The tankers called our commander and he sent a rifle squad out to take the prisoners back to headquarters. They took all the ammo away, but never got the rifle. When I stopped the gooks, I saw this last one throwing his rifle into the ditch. After they left, I went to pick up my souvenir—that rifle.

"Get some rest," Mosley told me. "I'll pull guard."

I lay down with my rifle and fell off to sleep.

I was awakened when I felt someone shake me. I looked up and saw a captain staring me in the face. "Do you have a rifle with you?"

"Yes, I got the rifle to take home as my souvenir."

"I have to take the rifle back to headquarters."

I never saw the rifle again.

That morning when we got back to our positions behind the hill, the guys were teasing me about capturing five gooks. I sat down with David and Frank to have our breakfast. We were sitting on a log facing the bend in the road as it went back into the valley. I thought I saw a gook peek around the bend then jump back as he saw me looking his way. I didn't say anything to the guys because I wasn't sure. Then I saw it again and I told them that I had seen a gook over by the road.

They laughed and said that I was spooked by the previous night's experience.

"Okay," I said. "Come with me and we will see." We walked over to the road and around the bend. Sure enough, this gook jumps out and raises his hands up over his head to surrender. We took him to our commanding officer.

"Get him some chow." We did and he sat with us to eat his breakfast.

So, you could really say that I captured six gooks that day. I was sure glad it was that way rather than them capturing our guys.

This was in November. Why do I remember? Because we had a full course with all the trimmings. The gooks must have smelled the turkey and they tried to ruin our dinner by shelling us with mortars. I crammed myself to the back of the bunker and ate all my meal. I have to admit, it would have been more enjoyable without all those rounds exploding on our positions.

Chapter 14

By Domenic

During the day, we'd go on patrols out in the valley. Joe Hoffman and I would take our squad out in the valley to see if the gooks were planting mines. One day on our way out, we came across a dead gook lying alongside the riverbank. He was fully clothed which made me suspicious. One of my men wanted to take a souvenir from this dead gook.

"Hey!" I yelled. "Don't touch that gook! Don't you know that he may be a booby trap? All you have to do is disturb that body and it may explode right in your face."

"I never thought of it. I'm sure glad you stopped me."

We moved further down the river and received some small arms fire from the gooks. We radioed back to our observers and they spotted the sniper. Our tankers returned the fire and I believe it silenced that sniper, or at least made him take cover.

On our way back to camp, we passed one of our tanks. Just as we passed, the tank fired its cannon. The blast from the muzzle almost knocked us over! Joe Hoffman went wild when he saw all those casings from the shells fall from that tank. "Boy!" he said. "I would sure like to come back after the war to pick up all this brass." Joe told me he was a junkman from Philly.

Speaking of Joe Hoffman, I had tried to locate him for many years, though not as hard as I should have. Thanks to another buddy who lived in the Philly area, some contact was made with the family. Although they were not very cooperative, they did indicate to us that a Joe did exist but had died an early age. We also learned to some degree of truth that Joe was severely sounded in Korea and had a metal plate in his head. This had just about left him a vegetable for his lifetime. I still would like to really talk to one of his children to get the real story. Joe Hoffman was a fine soldier and deserves much more credit than I believe he received.

One might ask: How can you be a friend to someone when you knew them a short time?

Time in Korea, in a combat company, is not measured by years, months, weeks, or days. In many instances, it is measured in minutes, if not seconds. That is all it takes; the minute you expose yourself to enemy fire.

So, to know a man for minutes, rather than months or years, is not unusual or uncommon when you sit in a foxhole on any hill in Korea. There were many men who I never even got to know their first names, yet they are my buddies for life. I can recall many faces of the men I was with, yet I cannot put the proper name to the face.

Joe Hoffman was, I believe, a character witness for the trail of Warren McConnell. Warren would be tried by military court for sleeping on guard duty in Korea.

I tried to get Warren to write to me. I believe that Warren owes a debt of gratitude to Joe and the others that were witnesses after his trial.

We met a few years back and it was really good to see Warren again after 35 years or more. I didn't see too much change in Warren as far as his physical condition. He was glad to see me, and we did expect to get together again sometime in the future.

Tonight Warren, Dale, and the rest of the men, would be going out on guard. I was up in my guard hutch, cold, as the wind was blowing across the valley. I crawled into my sleeping bag, just enough to keep my lower body warm. I slept with my sound-powered telephone glued to my ear. These phones had no ringers. You got someone to answer by whistling into the phone. Of course I don't mean a loud whistle.

The hours dragged on as we checked in every hour on our sound-powered telephones to our command post. It was around 3 a.m. and our phone check was in process to each position. I listened as each position checked in. One of our outposts, out in the valley, did not answer his phone. They tried a few times with no luck. We were immediately alerted, and a rifle squad was sent out to check. We thought that the gooks had over run that position. When the rifle squad got to the position, the lieutenant found all four guys asleep.

He poked Warren with his carbine and asked him, "Who is supposed to be on guard?"

"Me, sir," Warren said.

Nothing was done that night to the men in that foxhole. The next morning when they came off guard, I told Warren and Dale, "I believe you're in serious trouble."

They didn't believe so and thought all they would get was company punishment. Well, they were taken away that morning and I never saw them again. I did learn from home that Warren was being tried by a military court for sleeping on guard.

A few days later our medic, Doc Day, one of the best medics in the army, was supposed to meet a sergeant friend. They were going back to headquarters for a couple hours. The sergeant was standing at the bottom of our hill, calling up to our Doc Day to, "Come on down!"

Doc was working his way down when a gook 120mm mortar came in and landed right where the sergeant was standing. When the smoke cleared, the sergeant was nowhere to be found. It was like he had disappeared. We looked frantically with the Doc to find the sergeant. When the Doc found him, he was almost completely buried in a ditch, some 40 yards away. The Doc pulled him out and tried to give him aid. This guy was in no way going to survive his wounds. He begged the Doc to give him some morphine for he was in such agonizing pain. The Doc knew that you do not give morphine for the wounds that the sergeant had, but the Doc couldn't bear to see him suffering so much that he gave his buddy some morphine for his pain. The sergeant was removed to the aid station. He never made it and to this day, the Doc still blames himself for killing his buddy.

I talked to the Doc in recent years and the mention of his buddy brought instant tears to his eyes and he cried openly.

The scars of war are not always visible to the eyes. These are the hurts that many soldiers carry the rest of their lives. These haunting experiences happened when these guys were just young kids. How can they forget such horrible experiences that they witnessed at such an early age in their lives? Our liberal politicians should spend one day with our boys in a foxhole and they might understand what I'm talking about.

Chapter 15

By Domenic

November was coming to an end and we were preparing to move into another area for reserve. This new reserve area had the huge squad tents and we had the luxury of having a small pot stove to help warm up the tent. We picked out our respective tents and went in to place our gear down in the area that we would be sleeping in. Once we placed our gear down, we walked back outside. The very next tent was where our rifle platoon was to bed down. One of our Browning Automatic Rifle (B.A.R.) men went in to lay his equipment. He forgot to clear his weapon and when he placed the B.A.R. down on his pack, it fired off eight rounds that ripped through his tent and right through our tent—right where we would have been standing if we didn't decide to be outside at that time.

The company commander immediately issued an order to confiscate all ammo except for guard duty weapons. He didn't want any casualtics while in a reserve area.

This was one of the best reserve areas that we were ever in. The camp was decorated with pine boughs to give it a real Christmas atmosphere. The company commander issued an order that we should dress up the entrance to each tent with pine boughs and the best dressed tent would receive a prize. Doc Day took over the task of getting that doorway dressed up. The men pitched in and the Doc made our tent doorway as Christmas as you could get it, with what we had. The time came for the officers to judge and I must say that all the tents looked great. We were lucky and our tent won the first prize thanks to our Doc Day.

Some of the men celebrated while others sat in silence and dreamt of home. Christmas time or most any religious holiday away from home is difficult. The men couldn't help but wish they were anywhere else but in Korea.

It was nearing my eighth month in Korea and I'd soon be eligible for R&R (rest and recovery) in Japan. I had all the time in that I needed for R&R, but the army was behind in their schedule for the men going on R&R.

Chapter 16

By Domenic

It was near the end of December when I got my orders for R&R in Japan. I took all my gear and off we went by truck to Kimpo Airfield. We boarded an army transport with about 40 guys. We were off to Japan and very glad to get away from Korea.

We landed in Yokohama, Japan, and were transported by bus to Camp Drake. We went through a complete change from army combat to Class A uniforms right down to a haircut.

We were then sent to the mess hall for some real chow. I got my first taste of real fresh milk and real eggs, not to mention all the ice cream we could eat. After chow we drew an allowance and we were on our own for seven days.

Outside Camp Drake there were many cabs waiting for the guys. We got a cab and when it arrived at the hotel it was packed to the street with G.I.s. We thought, *To hell with this, let's go to Tokyo.*

When we asked the driver to take us to Tokyo, he told us he couldn't because there was a curfew in Tokyo for the G.I.s.

We laughed, then said, "What could they do to us? Send us to Korea?" We added that if he refused to drive us, we'd drive his cab to Tokyo ourselves.

He agreed to drive us, and we were off to Tokyo.

It was getting late and we wondered if we'd be able to get a room for the night. We asked the driver if he knew of a hotel that we could get a room in.

"Yes."

"Drive us there."

When we arrived, our driver went in to see if they had a room available for us. He came out and said, "Come on in."

We were met at the door by a young Japanese girl who instructed us to take off our combat boots. "No one is allowed in the hotel with street shoes on."

We took off our boots and were given slippers to wear. I was a little skeptical about leaving my combat boots in a rack in the lobby of the hotel.

The girl assured me that they were safe and not to worry. We registered at the desk with the mama-san. The hotel was immaculate and decorated for the Christmas season. I was with a Mexican kid from California named Abolonia Mezza. We ended up being the best of buddies.

We checked into our rooms and I got a real good night's sleep for a change. The next morning when I awoke, I couldn't believe I was safe and in Japan. We didn't know what the hotel would serve in the way of an American breakfast. I shaved and showered and that in itself was another whole new experience for me. I was standing in front of the sink shaving and in walks a young Japanese girl.

I was surprised and I yelled, "What do you want in the men's room?"

She just smiled at me and went about her chores as if I wasn't there. This was all new to me for I never saw this in the United States. After I finished shaving, I went down to the shower room. I stepped into the shower and was about to suds up, but the water was not flowing on my back. I looked around and there was this young Japanese girl holding her hand over my shower head.

I said, "What the hell are you doing?"

She said, "I'm making sure you have hot water."

The Japanese cultures thinks nothing of walking in on you when you are naked. It is a custom in Japan for whole families to join in bathing together in public bathhouses. This is probably why they are not the least bothered when they see a nude person.

After I was dressed, I went down to the dining room for breakfast. I ordered eggs with steak, toast, and coffee. I really wasn't sure what would be on the plate when it came out. It wasn't bad at all.

We were told after breakfast that the girls in the hotel do not sleep with the guests.

After the chow, we left the hotel to do some sightseeing on the Ginza. The Ginza is the main street in Tokyo, like Times Square in New York. We walked up and down the Ginza looking into all the store fronts. We had an American P.X., an army store for soldiers, on the Ginza where you could buy American or Japanese products. We also walked on the side streets to check the vendors. They sold everything from watches to clothing. We heard some commotion, looked up and saw a Japanese kid running at full speed right towards a vendor stand. Abolonia and I watched him to make sure he wasn't going to attack us as he came near. As he ran by a vendor's stand, he reached out and without stopping grabbed a fist full of watches. He disappeared into the crowd with the vendor chasing him. We left because we didn't want to become involved.

I think that we tried every bar along the Ginza. We had five days left and we wanted to make the most of them. Needless to say, I spent seven days in Japan and can remember very little of what I did in those seven days. But I can vividly remember some things that happened at our hotel like the mama-san having it decorated for the Christmas holiday and even playing American Christmas carols. One night, just before New Year's Eve, she had a photographer come in and take a picture of the group of men staying at the hotel. I couldn't believe my eyes when I saw the camera. It was the old cover-over-your-head-peek-through-the-lens-and-snap-with-a-flash-bar-for-light. It couldn't believe those cameras were still being used. I noticed that the guy with the flash bar was standing right below some hanging paper. I told the mama-san that the decorations would catch fire if he fired the flash.

She said, "Don't worry. It will be alright."

Well, the flash went off and the paper caught fire. We grabbed a fire extinguisher and put out the fire. The mama-san couldn't thank us enough for helping. With all the commotion we never did find out if a picture existed.

Our hotel was across the street from the GHU University and down the street from the Imperial Palace. Don't ask where the days went while we were in Tokyo. There were many days and nights that Abolonia and I never saw each other until we were back in our hotel. He would go his way and I would go mine. I guess when you go from bar to bar it is no different than if you were in the States. The only difference is the people. In all of the bars that we went into we saw the same arrangement for both the men's and lady's rooms. There is only one door for both to enter. Once inside, the men go to the right side of the room and the ladies to the left. There is really no separation between the rooms. At first, we could not get used to the idea, but after a few bars we got used to it.

A night out on the Ginza was just like being in New York City. Neon signs glowed on every building up and down the Ginza. People rushed up and down the street, going in and out of the stores. We even saw a Japanese play being staged right on the sidewalk. We watched it for awhile but couldn't figure what it was all about, so we moved on.

We had to be careful about the traffic. The Japanese travel on the left side of the road as to our right. So, when we stepped off the curb to cross a street, you had to look to your left rather than to your right like we were used to.

And the taxi drivers are unbelievable. They drive worse than the cab drivers of New York City. They seem to rely more on their horns than on their brakes. A few rides in a Japanese cab will be an experience you'll never forget. To make matters worse, their cabs were all old American cars from the 1940s; some even converted to running on steam. You would have to see it to believe it.

Chapter 17

By Domenic

The days seemed to fly by and now it was time to return to Yokohama. I was so drunk I don't remember much. I remember lying on top of a long table in a full room of G.I.s. The next thing I knew, someone was trying to wake me up. Our busses had arrived to take us to the airport. I was pulled off the table and onto the bus.

I was sleeping on the bus, and when I opened my eyes, I saw, through the front window of the bus, that the sun was just setting. I knew we were heading for the airport to board a plane, but have no recollection of seeing any airplane, let alone boarding one. The next thing I remember was I woke up and was looking around to figure out where the hell I was. There were other G.I.s sitting along the opposite side from us. I heard the drone of the airplane motor now. I looked out the window and saw all those snow-covered mountains below and said, "Oh, shit! We're back in Korea."

Our plane landed in Kimpo Airfield and our trucks were waiting for us. We boarded our truck and off we went, back to our outfits. It may sound stupid, but I was glad to see my buddies again. Fortunately, we were still in that same reserve.

It didn't take but a few seconds to get right back into the swing of things. We were told that they were going to have a U.S.O. show—a variety show provided for the troops— right in our camp. We were lucky to have Jan Sterling,

Paul Douglas, and a few others we didn't know of. Many men came to see the show. It was a cold, windy day.

Jan Sterling came out on stage in a light blouse and skirt. We were sitting in our parkas, freezing, and she was just wearing a light blouse. She finished her act by coming down off the stage, into the audience and sitting on the laps of a few guys.

The men loved the show. Though things happened very quickly in Korea; one minute you may be watching a show, and the next minute you're in a foxhole staring down or across the mountain at the gooks. So, our orders came down to move out. We had to have a full field inspection of our equipment. Each man spread all his gear out on his poncho for the sergeant to inspect. If any item was missing, it was to be replaced. Men usually lose equipment when they are on line. They might have been out on patrol and if attacked, they might have had to leave some items behind. Or when they got hit with mortar rounds, equipment was quickly destroyed. Of course, I'd rather see equipment destroyed than our guys.

Chapter 18

By Domenic

January 1952 we were getting ready for our next move. Our company commander told us we were going up on the Punch Bowl. All we were told was that it was the highest piece of real estate held by the allied forces in Korea. The day arrived and we climbed aboard our trucks. The ground was covered with snow and it was really cold as we rode the trucks to our destination. We pulled into an area with some squad tents at the base of this mountain. We got off the trucks and prepared to move out and begin our climb up. As we stared up to see the top of this mountain, we knew that we were in for some exhausting mountain climbing.

We got a short briefing from our platoon leader as to what to expect once we reached the summit. We began our climb, following our rifle platoons up on the trail. It was rather steep in some areas that there were rope railings strung along the trail to help us pull ourselves up through the slippery snow that covered the trail. Halfway up the trail I had to take off my parka, for it was getting too heavy for me to make the climb. So, I just slipped out of it and left it alongside the trail for one of our men to get it and return it to the supply tent.

Halfway up, the men were starting to feel their legs getting numb from the climb, and the weight of their equipment. Earl was just ahead of me on the trail. Following him was Torres, our 60mm mortar gunner.

Torres saw that Earl was having difficulty and asked Earl to give him his rifle to carry.

Earl looked around and said to himself, *If this kid, half my size, can make it, then so will I.* This gave Earl that extra strength to continue the climb.

After three or four hours we reached the peak of the hill. The next thing was to take over the foxholes with as little movement as possible so the gooks would not detect a change in troops.

It was just getting dark and we had to make out our guard list for the night. We haven't seen the other side of the hill yet and our guys were now in position in each foxhole. We set up our mortars with the aiming stakes for special targets out in the valley in front of our positions.

Lieutenant Wainwright set up our C.P. (command post) near our 60s; and our 57s were up on the top of the ridge line. Our C.P. was a bunker that had good protection from gook mortars. Morning came and we quickly did some forward observation of the gook positions across the valley from us. There was one finger that came up to our hill. Other than that, there was this huge valley separating us from the gooks. We zeroed in on our mortars—that morning—at targets in the valley that we thought the gooks might use to attack our positions. The first day up on the mountain, we checked all our equipment because it came up on a tramway built on this mountain because of its height. It would be almost impossible to make the climb to the top if we had to carry all our equipment. God only knows what our boys had to do to capture this hill.

We hadn't been up on the hill more than five minutes when Sergeant Vickers and Sergeant Baysinger both got their orders to rotate home. It couldn't have come at a better time. Lieutenant Wainwright called me to the command bunker and asked me to take over the mortars as the section leader. I really didn't want to leave my 57s because I had close relationships with my guys.

Lieutenant Wainwright insisted that I would do just fine in the 60mm mortars. Well, I was never the one to back down from any responsibility, so I was the new section leader of our 60mm mortars.

Frank Zachar thought I was crazy for leaving at this late time in our tour of duty with the 57s. Now I had the responsibility for three 60mm mortar crews. Thank God we had some of the best men who were on these mortars at the time. Most of them were my best buddies even before I took over the squads. One of the best was Roger Otterson, a seasoned veteran. He was one of the fastest gunners in our platoon barring none. We also had the four Bs: Burwell, Bullock, Bailey, and Burton. David was one of the squad leaders; Lavey as gunner; Earl Avers, gunner; Wendel Roberson, gunner; Truman Turner, assistant gunner; Dean Fultz; John Shelton; Homer Tomes; Torres; and Robert Tarr. Somewhere in our squads was a Wilks.

Of course, there were many more which their names escape me at this time. Lining up crews for a fire mission was easy as we were all very close to our gun positions. In the event of a gook attack our men would have to man each gun and fire when asked by our forward observer.

Our rifle squads would go down into the valley below on patrols every day. It was our job to give them supporting fire, should they request it. We had our targets all picked out and knew just where they needed our support. Each gun position had aiming stakes that were used to pick out certain targets in the valley below. All we had to do was to move from one stake to the next as they would call for support. It was not unusual for us to send a barrage out in front of our patrols to clear the way of any gooks. Even when they got ambushed, we could send many rounds out into the valley to protect our guys so they could get back up to our positions.

Days on this hill were never without something happening. Either we got incoming mail, or the gooks tried to infiltrate our lines. Each time our rifle squads went down into the valley on patrol, we usually got a casualty, or some killed. This one night, our patrol came back and one black guy was missing from the patrol. They said they had to leave him, for the gooks had them surrounded and had a hard time fighting out of the trap. It was a brutal cold night and they had to send another squad down into the valley to retrieve the body of our rifleman.

When they finally brought him up on the stretcher, he was frozen stiff as a board. So, if you didn't die from a bullet, the cold weather would claim you. The temperature up on the hill, with the wind blowing all the time dipped well below the freezing mark, sometimes to 30 degrees below 0. You can't stay out in that cold too long before you freeze. Even with the protection from the cold in our foxholes you must move yourself constantly while standing still.

One night a kid came back from a patrol and complained to me that his foot hurt. I looked at his boot and couldn't see any bullet holes or shrapnel. I told him, "Remove your boot." I looked at the boot real close at the back where the heel meets the boot. There was a little burp gun right between the heel and the boot. Lucky for him it was a burn gun shell, for it didn't have enough force to penetrate his foot. I told him that he had a million-dollar wound, but not severe enough to get him a ticket out of Korea.

The fourth day, I moved myself from one bunker to another, nearer to my 60mm mortars. Duncan, who was in my squad, took over my bunker. I had just taken all my gear from my old bunker to my new one. I turned around to see Duncan dive for the door of his bunker, just as a mortar round hit the top of the doorway to his bunker. Well, Duncan never got inside, and he was hit on his backside. We rushed up to help him. Our medic gave him a transfusion and patched him up. We sent him down by the tramway. I never saw Duncan again.

Thank God for this tramway built to get supplies up to our positions on the hill. If we had to carry the wounded off this hill it would be virtually impossible. The hill was too steep and the time it would take to make the journey down to the bottom would take too many hours.

When I saw Duncan dive into my old bunker, I couldn't help but think it could have been me. It may sound strange to hear me think like that, as if I was glad it was Duncan and not me. It is not unusual to think like this because we never knew who would be next and that we got another chance at life.

Of course, on every hill we have to have a latrine and this hill was no exception. Ours was between our two sections: the 57s and the 60mm mortars. It was just a hole in the ground with a box over the hole, with nothing around it for protection from the weather. I always noticed that it was rarely used during the daylight hours. If you had to use it, you must brave the cold as you brushed the snow off the seat to sit down on the box.

Now that I am writing about this latrine, I can never remember myself ever going to that one while up on that hill. Of course, it would be impossible to go 40 days without going to the toilet once. I am sure that I used it more than I care to remember. I do know that Lieutenant Wainwright would never come out during the day to use the latrine; I'd only see him at night. He was cautious about leaving the safety of his bunker.

Most of our days and nights were spent in our bunkers or foxholes because the gooks loved to shell our positions. There is no warning from a mortar round when it does come in on you. When you hear it, you can bet it is too late, for that last whistle is just seconds from the impact.

The most feared and deadliest is the mortar rounds from the gooks. To the G.I. it was instant death, or you were mangled for life.

A week went by and our company commander thought it was a good idea to blast a tunnel through the mountain. No one liked the idea, for the noise always attracted the gooks and they would return fire.

The blasting went on for a couple of weeks and at times Lee would try to hide Sergeant Wilkes so he would not have to blast that hole. Sergeant Wilkes would always find him, for there were not too many places you could go to hide.

All we heard for two weeks was, "Fire in the hole!" With all the blasting they only made a small opening in the mountain but never broke through to the other side. That mountain was solid rock and frozen solid. They finally had to give up on the tunnel.

One day David and I were standing out on the trail on the back side of our hill when I heard some men coming up the trail talking Italian.

I said to David, "Who the hell are these guys?"

When they came around the bend in the trail, we saw that they were black. We stopped them and found out they were the elite troops of the Queen and King of Ethiopia, stretcher bearers who were on our left flank, guarding an artillery piece of one of our outfits.

I said to David, "I am sure glad that these guys are on our side."

We had a huge bunker that we used for our men that came off guard duty to warm up and get some rest. This one kid had been on guard duty and was resting in his sleeping bag. He must have had a bad night out in the foxhole and crapped right in his sleeping bag. We had to get him out of there, and he had to clean himself up the best he could under the circumstances.

Fear of death takes on many forms for different people and his was not unusual. You would be surprised what your mind would let you do under extreme pressure. You will bet that no one thought it was strange for him to do what he did, and no one thought it was funny to joke about. No one can explain the feelings of the individual man as he faces almost certain death every day and night. No one complains and it is duty as usual as we go about our daily lives.

Chapter 19

By Domenic

The weather hadn't been getting any better as we continued to hold our position up on the Punch Bowl. Orders came down from headquarters that we were to draw for each man a week's rations.

The army brass came up with a plan to stop all firing of weapons along the whole 150-mile front including fire from offshore ships and aircraft. The army called it "Operation Clam Up."

Well, we all drew our rations and were informed to tell all our squads that no one was to fire his weapon under any circumstances—unless it was absolutely life threatening to our men. The men were to remain in their foxholes and not wander around in view of the gooks across the way from our positions. Movement outside the bunker would only be for guard duty change—and if you had to relieve yourself.

So here we sat for seven days without any artillery of any kind. It was frightening not to hear a sound after we were actually used to all the artillery exploding around us. After the second or third day we were getting a little paranoid and we began to wonder if we were left up here and everyone behind us had left.

Frank and I were on guard and as we sat in the wee hours of the morning, we saw two gooks walking along our barbwire as if out for a Sunday stroll.

Frank looked at me and took aim at the gooks with his carbine and said, "Hey, *Lom, I got them in my sight."

[*Editor's note: Short for "Lombardi"].

Yeah, Frank, but you can't fire so forget it, I thought and told Frank, "That is exactly why they are out there to draw our fire."

The gooks were curious and confused as to why we were as quiet as we were when before this, they never had a minute's peace from our artillery. We were supposed to remain like this for seven days. We were in the fifth day and as soon as it got dark everyone was on guard alert.

The weather got nasty as the wind kicked up and it began to hail. It seemed that the wind was blowing the ice pellets squarely into our faces. They felt like tiny razors cutting into your face and it was difficult to keep our eyes open. "Boy, Frank, this is great for the gooks. It seems like it's in their favor the way the wind is blowing!"

Somehow, we managed to protect our faces from those ice pellets and another day had passed. Day seven came and we were just about ready to forget our orders and resume our own war. Everyone was getting jittery with this silence, for we were not quite sure what would be next.

Then it came. Every weapon and artillery opened up at the same precise time on target. What a beautiful sound, after a week of silence. Once again, we were sure that we had our support behind us and a welcome back to the war with the support of all our rear artillery units. Thank God for them.

Chapter 20

By Domenic

Life resumed as usual after the orders came down. We were now ready for action with the gooks should they try to assault our positions.

I was with Lieutenant Wrainwright in the C.P. when I heard a thunderous explosion—something we hadn't heard before on this hill.

"What the hell was that?" I asked Wrainwright.

We checked with our C.P. and found out it was an artillery piece that the army had brought to the top of the mountain to fire point black at the gook positions across the valley from us. Every time this cannon fired, the whole mountain shook. And it shook when it hit the gooks' position across the way. This was good for us and it was also a calling card for gook artillery trying to locate it and knock it out of action. We were sure glad that this cannon was not aimed in our direction.

Every day the cannon fired into the gooks' positions and totally destroyed them. At night while we were on guard, we could hear them rebuilding them. This went on the whole time the men were up here for that operation which was called "Operation Bunkerbuster."

I found out many years later that this was the first time in this history of modern warfare a weapon of this magnitude was used on line with infantry troops and was considered a complete success. It took two bulldozers, one in front and one at the rear, to help pull and push this massive gun up on top of one of the highest mountains held by our forces.

Many years later I wrote a letter about the huge cannon we had up on the Punch Bowl with us the winter of January 1952. A fellow veteran saw the letter and wrote me. It seemed that this piece of history was completely forgotten at this time and I sort of brought it back to life for all to read. The fellow veteran assured me that the gun was real and to prove it, he was one of the crew members of that piece of equipment.

George Ellis had shown my letter to a buddy of his and he thought it was interesting and factual. He ended up showing it to some of his friends at a reunion.

A few years passed and I received a call from a Captain Arthur Wilson. He told me he had talked to George Ellis and he was interested in my letter for a book that he was in the process of getting published.

I never really thought the book would get to the publishing stage and I really had no reason to not allow the letter to be used in the book, so I told Arthur that if he needed more information to call me.

It wasn't long after that I did get a call from Arthur and he requested I review my letter for any errors or whether I would like to alter or change something. I sent the material back to Arthur and the book was out around the month of September 1996. The name of the book is "Korean Vignettes: The Faces of War."

Chapter 21

By Domenic

The U.S. Eight Army's howitzer from the 780th Field Artillery Battalion recently brought direct fire on enemy emplacements from the top of one of Korea's highest front-line mountains. Set on a self-propelled carriage of a 155mm howitzer, the eight incher's first assignment was the destruction of 40 enemy bunkers across the valley from the gun's position.

Captain Eric O. Gates, Goldsboro, N.C. operations officer for the eight incher's firing missions, explained that bringing the gun to the mountain top more than 1000 meters high was an experiment to determine the practicability and effectiveness of artillery "assault fire" in Korea.

From the gun's emplacement, the red's defensive positions were about 1800 yards away. Brig. General Harry M. Roper, a division artillery commander, noted the efficiency of the gun in knocking out bunkers and implied that the operation, tagged "Operation Mountain Goat" would continue to lift whatever burdens possible from the infantry-man's shoulders.

The 11-man crew, under the command of First Lieutenant Dennis Crafton, Roanoke, Virginia, volunteered for hazardous duty soon after the project was initiated. The honor of pulling the lanyard to discharge the first round was given to P.F.C. (Private First Class) William Butler, New London, Connecticut, an assistant driver and loader.

P.F.C. San Bran, Bakersfield, California, drove the massive vehicle through 12 miles of icy mountain trails into position. Bulldozers accompanied the vehicle throughout its climb, clearing the road and providing a winch when the slippery narrow road became steep.

Manning the highest fire direction center in Korea were Officer Captain Eric O. Gates and a crew of three enlisted men. Although most of the targets were visible from the gun emplacement, the fire direction center plotted each round with data provided by three forward observers.

For its first mission, the howitzer was assigned to eliminate 40 enemy bunkers. On the first day, 20 bunkers were destroyed with 107 rounds. When the reds observed the gun being brought into position, the dirt flew, according to the gun commander, Lieutenant Crafton.

Each round weighed 200 pounds and had a killing range of 30 square yards. Although the enemy bunkers were deep in the hillsides, faced with rock and reinforced with logs, each one chosen as a target crumbled before the howitzer's fire power.

My good buddy, George Ellis, was with that gun crew up on the Punch Bowl at the time our division occupied those positions. During the 26 days that gun fired on gook bunkers and other targets ranging from 800 yards to 3500 yards. The unit fired 2348 rounds at enemy bunkers and destroyed 160.

Little had been said about these two important operations. Thanks to my good buddy, Joe Russo, a med aid man with the 15th AAA battalion, knew of each.

The Punch Bowl had to be one of the most important pieces of real estate held by allied forces in Korea at this time. The men who took this hill and the men who held it from the gooks had to be commended as a fantastic feat of war. It certainly ranks high at the negotiating table with the North Koreans.

We spent over 40 days up on the Punch Bowl and came off February 26, 1952. Because of its height, most all heavy equipment had to leave by way of our tramway. The move had to be coordinated with the unit that was to relieve us. That meant that all their equipment had to come up to the top before we could send ours down. Our 60mm mortars had to stay in place until the new unit had theirs in our positions ready to fire if need be. Our 57s also had to remain in position until the new unit came in to occupy their positions.

With all this activity we had to remain very low profile so that the gooks would not detect that we were making a change of units. The night we were changing it was windy and very cold. All the men were instructed to bring their equipment down to the tramway as soon as they were relieved: "Leave the equipment and head down the hill to the waiting trucks."

It was a good couple hours down to the waiting trucks. I kept Earl Avers with me on the tram to help load the equipment on. We had our sound powered telephone to communicate with the men at the bottom of the tramway. At times, the wind was blowing so hard and it was so cold I could hardly hold on to the phone.

It was around midnight when we were able to start to send down our equipment. Earl loaded the tram and we were able to get all our equipment down to the waiting trucks. On the last load down, the tram operator asked if we would like the tram sent back up so we could ride it down.

I said, "No thanks." And Earl and I started down the trail about 1:30 a.m. We reached our camp around 3 a.m. and it was deserted.

I walked into the guard tent of the new unit and asked where Company B was.

They told me that the company moved out about an hour ago.

"Great," I said. *And they didn't have anyone to take us back with them.* I asked the guard to contact Company B and get Lieutenant Wainwright on the phone. I got the lieutenant and he sent a jeep out to pick us up.

When we arrived at our staging area all the men were sacked out on the ground and open gas cans were burning around the area to make it feel warm. Earl and I had just sacked out when we were awakened. We loaded on the trucks and we were off again to our new rest area.

We must have driven at least seven or eight hours to reach our next reserve area. The area was a treat, for we had the big square tents. We quickly cleaned them out and moved in for a well-deserved rest.

Chapter 22

By Domenic

February 1952, we were in a reserve surrounded by low lying mountains with a stream running through our camp. Captain Bray was our company commander. We were starting to receive a lot of National Guard replacements during this time. Many of them came with rank and it was difficult, at times, to give orders to some of them who held a higher rank than the men who were squad leaders. I was the section leader of our 60mm mortars at the time and only held the rank of corporal.

The two units were in separate tents. The 57s were in one tent while the 60mm mortar crews were in another. The kitchen tent was set up along the riverbank, while our tents were one behind the other, beginning with our 60mm mortar tent and so on, down to the company headquarters tent.

Life in reserve is not for rest, only because of all the new men we had to train. I couldn't believe that almost all the new men from the National Guard could not field strip an MI rifle to clean it. This was a basic necessity if you were to carry one into combat. You are responsible for your equipment to function if you care about surviving. This meant that we had a real job in training these guys before we had to go back up the line. Knowing how to field strip a rifle was just the beginning with these new replacements from the National Guard. There was much more to learn about survival while up on line. Every day we would take our respective squads out and drill them on the proper procedures in firing and maintaining the weapons they would be using. Training the new men all day gave them the necessary time for them to learn, for we never knew when we would be called back up on line.

Our platoon got quite a few replacements and our heavy weapons platoon received our share of them. This one old-time sergeant came to us and was placed into the 57s. At the time Frank Zachar was the section leader of the 60mm mortars. Well, after we were in reserve a few days, most men got to know each other pretty good. Usually the men would gather tree trunks and place them around our tents to dress up the area. Naturally when they trimmed off the branches, it left some wood chips on the ground.

Each morning all the men would fall out and we would have police call. The men would form a line and would move forward and pick up anything that was in their immediate front. This one day, as we did our police call, the men of the 57s were told not to pick up some tree limbs that were left by our men of the 60mm mortars.

Each section is followed by the section leaders as they make their way through the company area. I saw the men walk over the tree limbs and asked them to pick up the limbs, for they were not theirs. I went over to the sergeant and told him that they will pick up those limbs.

He got a little annoyed because I had no stripes on my uniform and wanted to know who I thought I was, talking to him like that.

I halted the whole police call and instructed the men myself to pick up the tree limbs.

At this time our new platoon sergeant heard all the commotion and came over to see what it was about.

The sergeant told the First Sergeant, "Who the hell is that guy to tell my men what to do?"

The First Sergeant told him, "You had better listen, for he is the section leader of the sixty-millimeter mortars, and he had been here long and is ready to go home in a few weeks."

That night when we were off duty, that sergeant came over to our tent looking for me. He wanted to become my friend and celebrate our friendship by offering me some of his whiskey ration. The last thing I remember was trying to get an M1 to go and shoot the First Sergeant. It must have been Frank and David who wrestled the M1 from me. Then I tried to jump into the river for a swim and Frank and David held me. I remember them dragging me up and down the company area to sober me up.

Well, they must have finally got me to stay in my sack, for the next morning when I woke up, they were laughing at how lousy I looked.

I asked, "What happened last night? All I remember was trying to shoot the sergeant and trying to take a swim."

Zach said, "You were out of it and we had a heck of a time trying to get you in the bunk to sleep."

Every morning before we went for training, I would go over to the C.P. and look at the list for my name to rotate home. W were supposed to rotate sometime in March. So, Frank and I were relived from training of the men and we would just go up into the mountains around the camp on patrols. This was the first time since we went to Korea, that we were relieved of the responsibility of being a combat soldier.

Zach and I would have our chow in the morning and would get ready for our journey up in the hills. We would always have with us a Korean—R.O.K.—soldier to bridge the language should we encounter any gooks.

I made an appointment with the dentist to have my teeth checked before leaving for home. I must have made at least three trips to the dentist and would always stop at the C.P. to check the list for rotation names. We were supposed to rotate home on the 15th of March, but our date was postponed for a later date, for some reason. So, Frank Zachar and I continued our patrols up around the mountains surrounding the camp.

As I noted previously, we had the best mess sergeant—Big Jim, as we all knew him. He made our meals as tasty as anyone could under the conditions. Big Jim was not only our cook but was also with us many times when we needed an extra rifle to fire at the gooks.

Most cooks in our kitchens were called to action whenever they were needed. And plenty of times they were. So, if you were a cook in combat company, you would invariably be called at some time or other to be a rifleman.

I must say that our kitchen was responsible for the morale of the troops. Men with a full stomach fight much better knowing that Big Jim would be there to serve them as soon as things became quiet.

Chapter 23

By Domenic

Frank and I got ready, as usual, to go up on our patrol. It was a nice, bright and sunny day as we made our way up a new trail. We were reaching the top of this trail when we heard a noise. We stopped to listen, and with our carbines ready we moved cautiously further up the trail. Frank took the left side and I walked the trail. As we got closer, we could hear someone moaning. As I rounded the bend in the trail, I saw someone lying along the trail in one of our sleeping bags.

I approached the sleeping bag with my carbine ready. I poked the carbine against the head of the person in that sleeping bag an asked, "What are you doing here?"

All I got from the person was a moan. On a closer look, I saw that the person in the sleeping bag was a girl.

I asked the Korean soldier to order her to get out of that sleeping bag.

He told her, but she moaned louder, and said, "I can't. I'm too sick."

I said to him, "Ask her what is wrong with her."

She was pregnant and experiencing stomach pain.

"Ask her what she's doing up here. And is she alone?"

She told the Korean soldier that she was with another girl.

I said, "Find out where this other girl is."

She pointed up the trail. We left her there and moved up the trail cautiously. A few hundred yards up the trail we came upon a small camp. We stopped and observed the camp for any movement. There was a squad tent set up, a fire going and a line of women's clothes hanging on a clothesline.

We watched for a few minutes. And then out walks this young Korean girl. We moved in immediately and questioned her. "What are you doing up here on this mountain by yourself?"

It was obvious, to us, that they had a little whorehouse going here.

I asked her, "Are there any Chinese troops or North Korean soldiers in this area?"

She assured us there were none.

I then told the Korean soldier to tell her that they must leave the area, or they will be taken into custody. We left the girls camp and continued our panel.

When we got back to our company area, we reported to our C.O. what we found up in the mountain. He immediately sent a squad of riflemen up to take them off the hill. I was kind of sorry for that girl in that sleeping bag anyway.

The men brought the girls down and turned them over to the Korean authorities. The men tore the camp apart and brought all the gear to our camp. When the company commander saw all the G.I. food that they had, he was furious. He had our whole company fall out and, in no uncertain terms, said he would not let this happen again while he was in command.

Chapter 24

By Domenic

March days were quickly passing and no word yet of our rotation on our bulletin board. Then one day after returning from the dentist, I stopped in front of the bulletin board and, well, could have heard me in New Jersey when I saw my name on the list for rotation home!

Zachars was on there also and I ran over to his tent and told him, "We're going home at last!"

When you get this close to going home, you become very nervous about going back up on the line. You feel that you have pressed your luck and it could be time it may run out on you. After three weeks, I knew we were getting ready to move back up on line soon.

March 21, 1952 was the day we were to leave the company. We got up early that morning and went to have breakfast with Big Jim for the last time. What a rotten day, for the wind was blowing the sides of the mess tent out and the snow and sleet were lashing at our feet as we ate our breakfast.

The time had come for us to say "good-bye" to our buddies. Here we are, ready to get out of there and feeling guilty for leaving our friends behind. The real problem was that we knew in a short time they would be going back up on one of those rotten hills.

I walked into our tent and most of the guys were still in their sacks asleep. I walked over to where David was and stood by his bunk. I didn't say anything and neither did he.

It seemed like hours. I couldn't get the words out and I knew that David had the same problem It was very difficult to say "goodbye" to our buddies. We had waited all these months to leave and now we were totally confused and feeling rather low. I don't believe we said one word to each other as I left the tent.

We boarded a jeep and I watched as we drove away from our company area. I was so down that I never spoke a word to anyone until we reached Inchon, Korea, three hours later. How do you explain your feelings to anyone on how it is to leave your buddies? If you never experienced what we went through together, you could never really understand our feelings. Who, but another combat soldier, could understand? To explain to the average person about combat is like a fisherman trying to convince his wife or friend of the "big fish he almost caught." If you weren't there or never had the experience, forget it. End of story.

Chapter 25

By Domenic

Arriving in Inchon, Korea was our first stop on our journey home. The camp was surrounded with a barbwire fence. A number of tents were inside the compound. The first priority was a complete physical and we stripped down to our shorts. We dumped all our belongings into our poncho and dragged them along as we went from doctor to doctor. The last place we ended up at was a long counter before you entered the delousing area to go into the shower.

There we placed all G.I. equipment on the counter for the army to confiscate from you. For many months I carried a small army knife on my belt. I kept it so nice because I had picked it up along the way one day as we assaulted a hill. To me, it was a souvenir of war. I tried telling this to the jerk behind the counter.

He wouldn't listen and I had to give it up. Boy, was I mad! It was a good thing that we were on our way home, for I would have kept it whether he liked it or not.

We moved on and got deloused and then headed for the showers. After the shower, we moved along to another area where they gave us a new issue of clothing and a duffle bag to carry all the new clothes. We had a good meal and now we had to wait for our ship.

In this harbor the tides drop some 30 feet, leaving the harbor nothing but mud flats. In order for us to leave this port we had to wait for the tides to come in and then we would board L.S.T.s, a landing craft for troops. The larger ship we were to board was docked out in the deeper water of the harbor. We did board an L.S.T. and it carried us out to the Sergeant Sylvester. They had four barges tied together to make a floating dock.

We got off the L.S.T. and boarded the Sergeant Sylvester for our journey to Japan. And finally, our next stop home.

We sailed down the Yellow Sea to the Sea of Japan. I watched as we sailed down the coast of Korea all the time thinking of the guys I had left behind. I was wondering what they were doing as we moved further away from the land of the morning calm, never to see it again. I had mixed emotions about leaving—glad and sad at the same time. I knew that our company was getting ready to move back up on the line very soon after I had left. I couldn't help but worry that some of my buddies would be in real danger then.

Soon we could not see any land and it was like a chapter of a book finished and we were on our way to the next. We saw the coast of Japan and glided into the port of Sasebo, the same port we left some nine or 10 months ago. Then back to the same camp we had been in prior. Now we had to wait for our ship that would take us across the Pacific Ocean, home to the United States.

Chapter 26

By Domenic

Sasebo, Japan is a seaport on the southern coast of Japan. From what I saw, it was used as a submarine base during the war. It was very clean and well designed to accommodate a large group of men. The barracks were built around a courtyard and they were equipped to serve your every need.

There were stores, barber shops, movies and recreation rooms all in our one unit. The camp was completely surrounded with a fence and was guarded by Japanese soldiers. We had no special duties at this time. So, when we got the chance we took off into the city of Sasebo.

Sasebo was known to be a swabby town, meaning a town for all the sailors. When we got there, the navy men didn't like the G.I.s messing around with their girls. The result was that there were many fights when we would go into town.

I happened to be with a guy from New York State named Alfred Lonzack. Naturally, the first thing you do is find yourself a bar to get some beer. This we did and we thought it would be fun if we took one of those bicycle taxis and drove it ourselves. We spotted a fellow sitting at the curb and I convinced hi to let me take the rickshaw for a spin. Alfred jumped in the back seat and we took off down the road with the Japanese taxi driver running behind. As we sailed down the main street, Al was standing up in the back waving his bottle at the people along the roadway. We were fast approaching an intersection and I would have to slow down or even stop if need be. I pressed on the brake pedal and it seemed to make the bike go faster. The harder I tried to press, the faster the damn bike went. I became alarmed because I would have to stop this bike somehow before we crashed.

I saw some hedges along the road and decided to crash the bike into the hedges to stop it. Thank God it stopped without any damage to us or to the bike.

At this time the Japanese driver of the taxi caught up to us and began waving his arms and shouting, "You broke my taxi!"

I assured him we didn't do any damage and handed him some American dollars. That shut him up like a clam.

Later I told Lonzack that the reason I crashed that bike was because I couldn't stop the damn thing. I told him, "Never again will I try that trick."

Sasebo, Japan was no different than any other Japanese city with overcrowded roadways and hundreds of people walking or riding along the main roads. If you were to ask me if I remember how the city looked, I am afraid that I didn't give it much thought at the time to be sight-seeing. We were there to have as much fun as possible before our ship came, and we would have to leave.

After that day, I never saw Alfred Lonack again. I often wonder if he would recall that day in Sasebo.

Chapter 27

By Domenic

As we waited for our ship to arrive in Sasebo, it gave us ample time to think about what we would be doing when we reached the United States. For many of us, it would be almost one complete year or more since we left the States. To many of us, the days seemed to drag as we waited for our ship. Remember, we had just come off the front lines in Korea and we were still not adjusted to civilian life as we once knew it.

Many were hardened to the core with hate for our government for sending them to this forgotten land. The men were asking themselves over and over again, "Why?"

What did we accomplish by killing so many of our boys? And not to mention the hundreds of thousands of North Korean and Chinese troops who lost their lives. Every night as we bedded down, we couldn't help but think about the friends we left back in Korea. We knew just what they were going through as they sat up on those windswept hills, never knowing when it would be their turn to get wounded or killed.

Yet, with all this behind us now, we were not yet thoroughly void of what our buddies would encounter night after night in Korea.

Word of a ship docking in Sasebo came down to us through the grapevine. Were we happy to hear this? You bet!

The name of the ship was General Miegs. It was capable of carrying over 5000 G.I.s.

Although the trip to Japan took just 10 days, this trip home was to take 18. No one really gave it any thought because who cared how long, as long as we were headed home.

Once onboard we were assigned our holds. I don't know why but they put me in charge of a Colombian Outfit. I was to monitor the men in my hold. I quickly found a good buddy who spoke Spanish and traded jobs with him. How was I going to keep all these Spanish speaking soldiers in line when I didn't understand their language?

I took fire watch up on the first deck where the cabins were. I went on fire watch from 3 to 5 a.m., sitting in the hallway where the cabins were. All I had to do was put on a white helmet, sit in one of the passageways for a couple hours, and watch for fires.

After watch I would go to the chow hall for my breakfast. I never had to wait in the chow line, for I had my helmet on for fire watch and we did not have to wait.

After that I had the whole day off until the next morning at 3 a.m. This was a snap and a good idea because I never had to wait in any chow line—which with 5000 guys is quite long. This gave me all the free time to hang out on the deck, take in the sun and shoot the breeze with my friends. Sometimes we'd play cards.

Strange as it may seem, the men were less gung-ho when we made this same trip going the other way. Most of the guys just sat around and did very little talking. I would guess that they were still thinking about their experiences in Korea and of the friends they left behind.

For some reason, you begin to wonder how the people back in the States will welcome us. As I lay on the deck of the ship, I recalled the days and months spent in Korea. I knew right then and there I had to make the transition from military life to civilian life. There were things I would have to forget and some things I would never forget. Of course an infantry combat soldier would like to forget some of the horrors, but the mind will not let him. He must learn how to handle those past experiences so as not to burden him the rest of his life. Unfortunately, there were many veterans from all our wars that can never make that transition to civilian life. I have found that over the years it seems to remain a stranger influence on your feelings and many instances of unhappy moments return.

I have to thank God that I made it home without any wounds, but for my buddies who were not as lucky. We are forever indebted to them.

For me and all the others that made it through the tour in Korea, had nothing, really, to do with God watching over us, for I am sure that God watches over all of us—even our enemy. It was nothing but luck and good training that helped us to survive.

There was a definite gloom floating aboard the ship as we crossed the Pacific Ocean. The men just lay around ton deck and there was very little playing around or joking going on, even though the cruise home was sunny and warm.

Early on the 18th day the captain announced over the P.A. system: "We are nearing the coast of California."

I was finished with my guard duty and headed for the mess hall for my breakfast. I wanted to make sure I was up on deck as we glided under the Golden Gate Bridge. I made a vow that I would be standing, looking up at the bridge the same as when we left California.

The California coastline became more visible and soon we were able to make out the Golden Gate Bridge. What a sight it was as we slipped beneath that gigantic superstructure. Everyone on deck let out a mighty cheer as the ship passed beneath the Golden Gate Bridge.

If you ever had any doubts about living in the United States, try visiting a foreign nation to see how they live. Then—and only then—will you appreciate what a great country you live in.

As we were being docked, there were hundreds of people waiting on the dock waving and cheering. The gangplank was hooked on and we were ready to leave the ship. As the army band played the men began to file down the gangplank to the dock below. Once the men were on the dock there was plenty of hugging and kissing as the parents, wives, girlfriends, family and friends met after many months.

There was a short ceremony on the dock. Then we were all bussed to the ferry boat that would take us across the bay to the waiting buses. The ferry boat was the Yerba Buena, the same one that carried us almost a year ago when we left for Korea.

After a short ride we arrived in Stockton, California, took the army buses to Camp Stoneman, California. What a great feeling it was to be back on American soil. We were given temporary quarters until we received our orders to go home. I was really excited to be back home and I knew that there were some of my buddies here in Camp Stoneman. I found out from some of the guys that Ted Convino, Louis Genefra and some others from New Jersey were in the barracks just a few blocks away. I decided to visit them before I went for chow.

I found the barracks and climbed the stairs to the front entrance. I opened the screen door and was just going up the stairs when I heard a voice shout, "Where do you think you are going, Soldier?"

Being away from a military base for so long I had forgotten some of the military rules. It was an officer and he said to me, "What do you say when you see an officer enter a barrack?"

I said, "You are supposed to yell, 'Attention!'"

He said, "What are you waiting for?"

I said, "Attention!"

And he got mad because I didn't say it loud enough. "Say it again and make it loud."

I then yelled, "Attention!" I heard all the guys upstairs jumping off their bunks to stand at attention.

The officer said, "That is better," and he walked out of the barracks. I then continued on up the stairs and all the guys were standing at attention.

When they saw me, they wanted to kill me for playing such a rotten trick on them. Thank God Ted Convino and a few others were there because I couldn't convince those guys that an officer was downstairs and made me do it.

The next morning after chow we all fell out for a formation. The First Sergeant had a list in his hands. The moment had come, for now we would get our orders and board the train that would whisk us home to New Jersey.

The First Sergeant announced that some will fly home and the others will go by train. Then he walked down the line of men standing there and cut the line of men right at my spot in line. He then said, "From here down, you will be flying home. The rest will get ready to board the train."

What a break to be flying home. If we had to take the train ride, we wouldn't be home for at least four days. We got our duffle bags and were taken to San Francisco Airport. We boarded a small twin-engine plane operated by a company that called themselves the Flying Tigers. It didn't hold too many guys and I was beginning to worry about taking this airplane ride.

We took off from California and landed in Tulsa, Oklahoma for gas and a bite to eat. We were off again and this time we landed in Tennessee. We didn't stay very long and we were on our last leg of our journey home— destination North Philly Airport.

When we approached New Jersey, we ran into some severe thunderstorms. "Oh, God!" I said. I had just spent all that time in Korea, traveled across the Pacific and across the United States and now I found myself in danger of getting killed. The storm was really in full fury as we looked out the windows of our plane. We saw huge thunderbolts of lightning which lit up the sky like it was daylight.

The stewardess came back and told us to fasten our seat belts. The pilot was going to land the plane and now it was so quiet you could hear the guys breathing. We felt the plane descending and we all waited for the wheels to touch that runway.

At last we were down and everyone on board gave a yell as the plane rolled down the runway to a stop.

We boarded buses for a trip to Camp Kilmer, New Jersey. It was early evening and we had some chow and then we waited around for our orders to leave. Camp Kilmer was not being used that much by the army and it was practically deserted. We had to sleep over night and the following morning we received our orders to go home.

The army doesn't provide any transportation from this post. Most of the guys called home for someone to come pick them up. One of my buddies called his parents to come for him and he offered me a ride to Penn Station, Newark.

When I reached Penn Station, I was going to get a bus for home. A cab driver pulled up and asked if I needed a ride.

"What the hell," I said. "I might as well ride home in style."

The cab took me right to my front door. No one was expecting me for at least a week. They didn't know that I was lucky enough to get a flight home.

I walked up the back steps. My family was really surprised to see me. We talked a little and my mother wanted me to call my father at work—and Toni.

I said it wasn't necessary because I would be home the whole month and would have plenty of time to visit.

Chapter 28

By Antoinette

It was about 11 months before I saw Domenic again. The first letter he wrote me from Korea, he wrote, "It seems like years since I've seen you" and that he hoped to be a "perfect husband."

We wrote each other almost every day and I still have a box of over 200 letters. I sometimes sent him stamps for letters. I also sent boxes of pepperoni and canned goods. His army mates all loved pepperoni. Domenic said he made a lot of friends sharing.

My letters to Domenic had to be burned so they wouldn't get in the hands of the enemy. Some of the things the enemy could have done would be to scare the family. Domenic told me most of the guys got rid of the letters. Others took a chance holding on to them.

Domenic couldn't believe he was in the army, which he felt was as bad as serving time in jail. He had very long days, from 4:50 a.m. to 6 p.m. Some days he got up at 3:30 a.m. and was marching by 4 a.m. with a full pack on his back, out to the firing range. Every night he had to clean his rifles and he had rifle inspection.

He slept with that rifle, even took it to the toilet with him. Any time he walked away from his tent his rifle had to be with him.

Domenic wrote that they had to clean their rifles, get clean linens, shave, make beds, shine their shoes, mend their clothes, take a shower, and rearrange their footlockers in order to get ready for the next morning's line-up.

He wrote that my letters to him made him cry and he thought of me constantly. He was also homesick. Being in the army, he said, was a good place to concentrate on me, because he had a lot of time. He had written that he wished we had gotten married.

It rained and flooded a lot in Korea, which made Domenic very depressed. It was also very cold and damp. The soldiers were always outside, in the front lines, with the exception of their tents.

In my letters to Domenic, I shared that I was worried he'd marry someone else while over there. I was young and didn't know. They were in the front lines…who would they meet? But Domenic reassured me in his letters, and how much he loved me. I just wished the war was over and he'd be coming home, but the future was uncertain. I just had to wait and see. I continued my life as it was going, working and seeing my girlfriends. If Domenic was coming home, it was up to God.

During the month of August 1951, Domenic became a private, but it wasn't a big deal to him because he wasn't anxious to be in service. If he intended to make a career out of being in the army, it would have been a big deal, but he couldn't wait to get out. He said that the army is alright, but not for him.

Occasionally in the reserve area, the soldiers would get to see movies to take their mind off the war. One of the movies Domenic had seen was "Appointment of Danger" starring Alan Ladd. He also saw a big show featuring Jack Benny.

Near the end of August was the first time Domenic saw bombing and strafing, which is airplanes firing machine guns. He never saw that before in person, only in the movies. It was exciting, "Something to see," Domenic said. The planes came right over his head. Domenic said the guys used to say that the married pilots were cautious. The single pilots took more chances. No one knew for sure, but that's what they would say. It was two months that Domenic was in Korea and he still hadn't fired his rifle. He was glad about that. He only fired it in Japan to make sure his equipment was up to par and that he knew how to use it. The rifle was more his protection in case he needed to safeguard. He used 60mm mortars, bombs with an explosive head, fired from a tube.

Mortars from the enemy landed all around them. "Fortunately, not close enough," Domenic told me. "Naturally you're concerned about getting wounded or killed. You have a job to do."

I couldn't wait for the war to be over, so I could see him again. We wanted to make plans for our lives, like getting married, buying a house with a white picket fence—The American Dream—and having children. Nothing is as exciting as having your boyfriend sitting next to you, but I killed time working and going to the movies.

The last time I heard from Domenic, for a while, in September 1951, he told me that there was an article in the *Stars and Stripes*, a military newspaper, that a girl wrote her stationed boyfriend a letter from song titles. Domenic thought the letters I wrote him would end up in a newspaper too if anyone saw them because my writing was "so good."

Domenic also wrote that he was fed up with war and travel. He had seen enough of the world already and wanted to be home where he belonged. "When I come home, it will be for good," he wrote. "I will be satisfied with living in New Jersey."

From September to November of 1951 I thought something happened because I didn't hear from him. But I put it in the back of my mind that he might not be coming back.

When I finally got a letter in November, I had to immediately write back that I was happy he was okay. I forgave him; he was up in the front lines.

By now Korean soldiers were surrendering. Domenic shared that "the smart ones, the ones who want to live," surrendered and were put in an area with prisoners. "We made sure they ate and were healthy. Then we put them in a prisoners of war compound, five or six miles behind our lines. They loved it. They were free. Their worries were over."

Domenic had a new job, an assistant gunner on the 60mm mortar. He'd drop the rounds in and fire them.

Meanwhile, back at home, my sister and I saved money and brought my mother a TV. This was the first TV we had. It had a small screen, 12 or 13 inches. She was so happy to get it and we stuck it in her living room. Of course, The Korean War was on television.

By writing to each other, I felt we grew closer; close enough to share with him that I once put my girdle on inside out! The other soldiers wondered what Domenic was laughing about when he read my letter.

And his letters were just as honest. In one he wrote: "I just want to know that you pull down the shade at night and you watch the way you sit around people. You remember you used to get a little careless at times. I want to be the only one to look at your legs."

Domenic shared his jealousy via letters a few times. I had sent him poems he felt were "dirty" and he hoped I got them from the girls at work, not another fellow. In another letter he told me that in one photo I looked "drunk."

In Korea, Domenic missed the American cars and it was a long time since he seen one. He wrote home and asked his family for a picture of their car. He was not comfortable in that environment, which was entirely different from what we do. "You have to go with the flow," he said. "In Korea, they traveled by two-wheel carts and foot. Most of the families there were poor, from what I saw. They were lucky they had food to eat. Maybe in the cities I'm sure there were cars, but where we were in the country, they were back a hundred years. They were content just to be living. What they don't know won't hurt them; they probably only traveled ten miles from their house. I doubt they had TV when I was there. They might had had radios."

Domenic had a Korean friend who fought in the U.S. Army who was in his platoon. Domenic tried to teach him words in English and he translated them in Korean for him, as he could only understand a little English. "Korea was fighting Koreans. It was a dumb war," Domenic said. "It didn't make any sense. They were sure glad we were there. They learned a lot from us. They didn't know what freedom was until we got there."

Domenic shared with me, too, that he would miss his buddies when he came home from the army, as they lived together like brothers. He imagined he'd feel a little down-hearted leaving them and coming home and that it would take awhile to forget them.

Chapter 29

By Domenic

Just hearing from home, in those letters--what Antoinette was feeling--it was an attachment. Probably as close as you're going to get from home for a while. So, when I returned home from Korea and saw Toni for the first time it was surreal.

Toni arrived at my house. I was sitting on the radiator in the kitchen where I could see the front door. Toni walked into the living room and just stopped. I got up from the radiator and went into the living room and threw my arms around her.

I guess Toni was still in a state of shock and just couldn't believe that I was home.

In the days that followed we did a lot of visiting. It was great being home for those 30 days, but how fast they went! Soon I would have to report back to my outfit in Fort Meade, Maryland. I wasn't finished with my tour yet and I would have to stay in until October 1952.

Chapter 30

By Antoinette

When I first saw Domenic after 11 months, I stopped short and didn't move. I was in shock! I was even afraid to go near him after such a long time. At first, he looked different to me and I was afraid he wouldn't feel the same about me, even though I felt the same about him. And I just couldn't believe he was home. Domenic got up and came to me, as I stood in the living room. He threw his arms around me and we hugged and kissed. When he noticed that I cut my hair, he was furious. He told me I looked "terrible" and didn't look like the same person. Shorter hair was easy to take care of, but he said, "What's wrong with you? You know I like long hair." I started growing my hair back to make him happy.

In the days that followed, we did a lot of visiting before Domenic would have to report back to Fort Meade, Maryland. We spent some time alone and we talked alone. He didn't speak much about Korea, but he wanted to know when we'd get married.

He got me a diamond that was a carat and 30 points with a white gold band. Today it's worth $10,000 because it's an antique. We were officially engaged May 1952 and had a reception at the Veterans' Recreation Center, West Orange.

It was hard when he had to leave again, but being stationed in Fort Mead, Maryland he was able to come home on weekends.

Chapter 31

By Domenic

I didn't want to lose Antoinette, so I proposed to her. She was surprised. I didn't want to go back to Fort Dix and leave Antoinette, but I had to. I had no choice.

I arrived in Fort Dix around June 1952 to finish my tour of duty.

It was during the Korean Conflict that Truman had implemented his plan to desegregate the armed forces. While stationed at Fort Meade, Maryland, I saw that the army was still segregated. I watched as the new recruits came in for processing. They were mixed as they entered the building. And when they were marched away, the whites were all together and the blacks were marched off to a separate area of the base.

It was very difficult for the black Korean vet to walk around outside of our company area while with his white buddy. It wasn't accepted here for the two races to be seen together. Being raised in New Jersey, I attended schools with black kids. The only thing that I knew about segregation was what I read in our history books. I couldn't believe what I saw while down in our nation's capital. Signs on all restaurants, water fountains, and bathrooms that read: "Whites only."

My first pass in Fort Meade found a bunch of buddies heading for Eat Baltimore Street, which was similar to what Times Square was in New York. It was a real wild strip with many bars, strip joints, and movie theaters. Naturally our first stop was a bar.

I opened the door and was about to step inside when I heard the bartender yell, "Where do you think you guys are going?"

I had no idea that the bar was segregated and told him we wanted to get drinks.

He said to me, "It's okay for the white fellows. But those blacks will have to go next door to their own bar."

I was not only embarrassed I was really mad to think that my buddies couldn't even have a drink with us. We decided not to go into that bar and to look for another. My black buddies felt it was useless and that we would not be able to go anywhere as it would only cause trouble for us to all be together. So, we had to split up if we wanted to move around freely.

I couldn't help but feel *this is just plain crazy*. Only a few months ago these same men were over in Korea willing to give up their lives for these same idiots that refused them to enter the bar and have a drink with their buddies. Now, Baltimore is about 300 miles from where I was living in New Jersey. I really couldn't believe that only 300 miles away there was a whole set of different rules that the black man had to live by. These boys donned a U.S. Army uniform and went overseas to a foreign land to protect the rights of that individual so he could refuse them entrance to his bar. We never questioned sending our black men to war with the white man. Those enemy bullets and mortar shells never could distinguish between a white man, like me, or Sergeant Henry Lewis, who was my black squad leader.

Even in the past in Fort Meade, Maryland, there was a double standard with the black soldier.

Chapter 32

By Domenic

With all the bars and strip joints in Baltimore, such a place was loaded with girls waiting to pick up a G.I. You soon learned that the pimps work in the bus depot and the streets in East Baltimore. As soon as a bus pulled into a station, the pimps would try to get you to pay them for the pleasure of one of their girls. If you were foolish enough to consent to their wishes, you would never see a girl or your money or that guy again.

One night, Richard Stalling and I decided to go into Washington, D.C. When we got off the bus, sure enough, a pimp approached us. I said to Rich, "This is a scam. Let's play along and see what he's up to."

The pimp told us not to walk with him because the cops were watching. We followed close behind and when he stopped and went into an apartment, we were to wait in the hallway until he waved us on. Once we were in the hallway, he demanded money up front.

Rich told him, "We have to see the girls first."

The pimp said, "I can't do it that way." We had a feeling he knew we were on to him because now we saw another guy coming from the back hallway. The pimp then took off for the front door and the other guy ran out through a side door. We chased them for a block before we spotted a police patrol car coming.

We stopped chasing the guys and a cop in the patrol car asked, "Is everything alright?"

We told the police we were okay, and they pulled away.

Today when I stop to think about what we did that night, I can't help but wonder if it happened today, would you have found Rich and I dead in that hallway? Thank God we can look back on some of the foolish and dangerous things we did and be grateful to be alive. The thought of what might have happened sends chills up my spine.

After a week in Fort Meade, I wanted to get myself a car to make the journey home on weekends. Of course, I still missed Antoinette. Being in the army, you just can't take off when you feel like it. So, you stay there and brood. But being in Fort Meade, you had a little more freedom—not that much freedom though. Still, it was a refreshing change from Korea.

Chapter 33

By Antoinette

I was happy to see Domenic more often during his time in Fort Meade. He had a car that he brought from his brother-in-law; it was a Buick. We'd visit our friends, go to the movies. We enjoyed each other after not seeing each other during that time in Korea.

During the week I still went to work and spent time with friends. There wasn't much to do, but we bowled. It was boring all week without Domenic, but we were able to talk on the phone every day. Since he came home on weekends, we didn't write like we did in Korea.

We weren't making wedding plans yet; we were still in the courting stage and celebrating our engagement.

During one of his trips back to Fort Meade he fell asleep at the wheel while going over a bridge. He was simply tired from all the traveling. It was over a three-hour ride. He wasn't injured but after that incident, his mother told him not to come home on weekends anymore. Mothers worry about their children.

Dom and I discussed it and he said, "Don't worry about it, I'm still coming home."

Another time he ran out of gas on his way back and I had to meet him to give him money for gas. It was about an hour away. I gave him a big hug and kiss and told him I'd see him again on the weekend.

Chapter 34

By Domenic

I made friends with a sergeant of our platoon, Sergeant Balicki, a big Polish kid from South Amboy, New Jersey. He had been in the Merchant Marines and was drafted into the army. Every day when all the men fell out for work detail, Sergeant Balicki would never pick me to go on any work details. During the day we would have big card games in the barracks.

At night, after chow, we would ride into a small town in Maryland called Glen Bernie. It was here in Glen Bernie that I was first introduced to the frosty beer. The bar kept all the beer glasses in the freezer and when you ordered a beer the cold glasses were filled, giving you a frosty glass.

They also had gambling machines in the bars. For the first time, I saw a machine that paid back real money. Naturally you always end up losing more than you would win.

One night all the guys piled into my car and we headed for town. We decided to crash this hillbilly dance. After a few hours of drinking, things began to get rough. Guys were getting whacky and fighting. They like their moonshine down there. We had enough and decided to leave before we got involved.

We piled in my car and headed back to camp. Everyone in the car was fast asleep and I was having a hard time keeping my eyes open myself. I eventually did doze off and when I woke up, I saw the traffic light and a car in front of me stopped for the light. I slammed on the brakes and slid into the car, knocking him into the intersection.

Joe Faciponti was sitting up front and hit his head on the windshield. He never woke up.

A gentleman in the other car got out of the passenger side and slowly walked around the car to assess the damage. He looked in our car and saw a bunch of G.I.s—none moving—and turned away, went back to his car and drove off.

I still don't know how I managed to keep my eyes open for the rest of the trip back to base.

The next morning when we went for chow, I saw the damage from the accident. The front fender on the driver side had my license plate embedded right into the fender.

"Hey, Lom, how did I get this bump on my head?" Joe asked.

"Don't you remember? I hit a car last night."

He said he didn't remember anything.

Of course, we laughed about it, but it could have been a lot worse.

After chow we went back to our rec room. There were a couple guys playing table tennis. This one guy had red hair and he was a pretty good ping-pong player. We started a conversation and I asked him where he was from.

He told me, "Chatham, New Jersey."

I lived in Orange, which wasn't that far. His name was Joseph Benneduce. We played a few games of table tennis. He won with no trouble.

Sergeant Balicki sent word down that he wanted me up in the barracks. I went up to our meeting room and Ballicki said, "Come on, Guinea, we got a card game going." We played for hours as each player ran out of money. These games would have, at times, $200 or $300 in the pot. You had to win a few times in order to stay in the game. The game would come to a close when the losers felt that they had enough.

On weekends, most of the guys liked to go home on a pass. No one really ever tried to get a pass. We knew that the army had roll call every morning. So, when a guy felt like going home, he would tell his buddy that he was staying on the post to answer for him when his name was called. The sergeant called off the roster and he checked off all the names of the missing. We usually returned on a Sunday night. The next morning the sergeant never made the usual roll call. All he did was read all the names that were missing at the previous roll call. He told us to form a line in front of the company commander's office. There must have been at least 75 guys. We each went in front of the C.O. and he gave us the punishment he thought we deserved.

I pleaded guilty and was court-martialed with the loss of a stripe. I almost got into more trouble when I told the C.O. that he could have the other stripe for another 30-day leave. Fortunately, he was a Korea veteran and he let it ride.

This one day I got caught for a detail. I got on the ack of the truck with the rest of the men. Off we went down the road and every time the truck would stop a stop street some of the guys would jump off. When we got to where we were supposed to work there wasn't enough guys on the truck. The next time they sent a military-police along on the back of the truck to watch the men.

I had two prisoners that were supposed to cut some grass. I sat up on the top of the lawn and watched as these two guys pushed their lawnmowers. This one kid was really moving with little or no effort while the other guy was really puffing. I looked closer and saw that this one kid had his mower turned up and was never cutting the grass. I called to him and said, "Your mover isn't cutting, maybe you should try turning it over."

He said, "It is a lot easier to push this way."

I had to laugh to myself and let him go.

Chapter 35

By Domenic

The time was nearing when I would be finishing my tour of duty in Fort Meade. Little did I know, my buddies would be thrown into one of the greatest conflicts of the Korean War. Almost to the day that I was leaving Fort Meade for home discharged from the army, John Shelton and Dean Fultz were among the many men of the 32nd that were wounded in the Battle for Triangle Hill, October 1952.

Based on what we had done in Korea, can there ever be a closure, an end to the memories we have to carry the rest of our lives? Were we war heroes or pawns of our government? Did we ask to go to Korea? Did we refuse to serve in Korea? Did we ever complain about Korea? Did we demonstrate against our government for sending us to Korea? Did any of us run off to a foreign nation keeping us free of serving our nation? Did we ever hear anyone burning his draft card? Did we go back to our civilian lives right from service? Did any Korean veteran ever put pressure on our government for compensation of any kind?

I have to admit, that besides all the commotion the Vietnam veterans acted out, they did lead the way for the politicians to take notice of the veterans. Yeah, they squawked loud and long and they got their Vietnam memorial in Washington, D.C. Then they didn't rest there; for now, they wanted a memorial right here in New Jersey for the Vietnam veterans. With enough support from the veterans of Vietnam they succeeded in having their memorial erected on the Garden State Parkway in Holmdel, New Jersey.

Korea was not a very popular war as we must all understand. It was only a short time ago that we had just came out victorious in a world war. That was 1945 and everyone was relieved that all the killing of our men and the destruction of cities around the globe had finally come to an end. Our post war years were left to building our economy and finding homes and jobs for all the returning veterans. So, 1945 to 1950 was just a few short years and most of the world was getting used to peace.

When Korea emerged, no one would dare say, "War in Korea." They didn't want to believe, so hence we became the "Police Action Forces in Korea." It didn't sound bad and the people believed we were in a police action in Korea.

Truman, with his political cronies kept the American people unaware of what was really going on in Korea. Our TV media was fairly new, and it was not in the best interest of our nation to broadcast the war in Korea.

I can remember it like it was just yesterday. I was working my job after quitting my senior year of high school in 1947. All was going fine until 1950. The Korean Conflict (or Korean Police Action) was the talk of my place of employment. Little did I know that just a few months later I would be part of that mess in Korea.

A fellow employee that worked in my department had a marine son who was in that Chosen Reservoir deal. We listened to him tell how bad it was for the marines in

Korea. Believe me; no one thought he was telling the truth. Everyone said the same thing, "It's just a police action. What is this guy talking about?" A few months later I got my draft notice and found myself inducted into the army— Jan. 21, 1951.

I will have to admit that I was very wrong in thinking Korea as a police action. Of course, I never did find out until the day I landed in the port of Pusan, Korea. My thinking at the time was excitement. There I was, thousands of miles from home in a foreign nation— actually elated. Wow! I never traveled more than 50 or 60 miles from home.

But then the bubble burst. I got my first indoctrination— the dropping of a real live ammo on our outfit. That scared the living hell out of me. I made it a promise to myself that I would never forget—this isn't a policeman's job; we are combat soldiers ready to give our lives. For what?

Originally printed in *National Veterans News,* October 2006

By Domenic Lombardi

I don't think I'm a bad boy or a hard ass. I was just 18-years-old, going on 19, when I was in Korea. With very little knowledge that I had at the time and my immaturity, my government asked me to do what the medical profession wouldn't even touch with a 10-foot-pole, not to mention the insurance companies. I was just an 18-year-old kid playing "doctor." And God only knows how many times a split-second decision had to be made and under enemy fire.

Our wounded boys lying there and looking up at you as if they were conscious with all the horrendous things that war can do to the body. Staring up at you, they plead, "Please save me." Their eyes telling me the hurt they must have.

Because so-called adult leaders of our nation can't solve the problems, they send our kids to fight for them. Most times many of them killed, maimed for life or missing forever in action.

Two days before I was to rotate, my battalion sergeant decided I should go and help dig G.I.s out of the shallow graves—a sight that will remain forever in my mind. It was a horrifying, shocking experience to retrieve the bodies of our soldiers from these shallow graves. The soldiers were bound with their hands behind them and shot through the head.

Who gives a damn in this country? All we see here in the good old U.S.A. is "Me, me, me and my SUV with my cell phone stuck in my car." When we had the last storm didn't you see all the people panic and run out and buy bread and milk? How would you like to have these people next to you in Korea in a battle? No way.

When I think back, what did you have in Korea for comfort? Nothing. Okay, if you received mail from home...great. Some guys had no one at home to write them, let alone a girlfriend. So, what did you have? Combat, lousy weather, war related diseases and the land of the dead. You also had loneliness, fear, stomach cramps and the runs. Then the loss of many good buddies because we were going through the sentence your country imposed upon you for being a good American.

The war has been over for more than 50 years and we know because we were there. Our young American school children have never been taught that we were at war in Korea. I would venture a guess that many don't even know Korea existed. If you don't believe me, look in our high schools' history books that we pay taxes for—Korea's not there. At least not the way we experienced it.

I don't care a damn about visiting Korea. It's a bad memory for me and it gets worse every day, especially with the attitude of the so-called Americans of today. This country will never be like it was during World War II or Korea ever again.

All you members of our veterans' organizations around the USA please take note. I am no war hero by any stretch of the imagination, but I have seen my full share and it will remain with me the rest of my life. I wouldn't even venture a guess on the magnitude of hurt suffered not only on the battlefield but for the rest of these medics' lives. It is no doubt in my mind that a combat medic would or should be considered a prime candidate for post-traumatic stress disorder—no questions asked.

Thank you, guys, we love you all.

Letter to the Editor, by Domenic, printed in local paper

Dear Editor:

True, we live in a society that has enjoyed peace and prosperity, surely earned by the men and women of our Armed Forces. Many who served; sacrificed their lives and limbs. Forgotten are the men and women who fought in the trenches of World War I, who suffered mustard gas, bullets, bayonets, and fragmentation rounds, while here in the U.S. we enjoyed peace and prosperity. Two decades later, a lunatic decides to conquer all of Europe. Yes, our soldiers were sent to defend the world's freedom. They went with the determination to win and win they did. All the time, we at home enjoyed peace and prosperity. No one likes war, but it does bring prosperity to our people building our war machine. Once more, our army was sent to defend the South Koreans from their brothers to the North. We went, and after three years of bitter fighting, a truce was signed. Yet back home, our people were enjoying the same peace and prosperity.

Vietnam! Who can forget? It was the longest drawn out war in our history, not to mention the notoriety it received from draft-dodgers and many demonstrators. Let's not forget Grenada, Panama, Beirut, Desert Storm, Somalia, and now Bosnia. Why should we ask our army to be put in harm's way for a nation that shows very little respect for the military?

I have been a resident of Livingston since 1953. I have viewed many, if not all, the Memorial Day parades in Livingston. While many did observe Memorial Day as a solemn tribute to our service men, many just saw it as a day off from work with pay. Today we are straining at the moral fabric of our society. Where is the patriotism? Are we really sure that by removing prayer from our schools helped? Will removal of the pledge to our flag be next? Our nation is overrun with illegal aliens draining our resources and adding much to our internal strife. This should be a warning of what is yet to come. All the liberal anti-war beatniks who pride themselves in spewing out anti-American rhetoric never stop to think it was these veterans who gave them that freedom to enjoy.

Let's not forget that the veterans of all our wars gave you this day to pay tribute to the men and women who made the supreme sacrifice—not just a day off with pay. If the parade is too much of an expense, I suggest you go to work and give back to your employer his day.

I served in Korea and am proud of it. If asked, I would do it all over again. I am proud to have served and proud to be an American.

In the News (and in scrapbooks!)

By editor, Maryanne Christiano-Mistretta

Antoinette kept two meticulous scrapbooks full of hundreds of photos, memorabilia, and newspaper clippings during the time Domenic fought in the Korean War.

Creating these massive scrapbooks kept Antoinette busy as she waited to hear from Domenic during his time in service.

Even though the giant scrapbook has enough to spark so many memories, Domenic said, "There are some things you'll never forget."

Domenic was mentioned many times in the *Orange Transcript,* including winning the Combat Infantryman Badge and the Korean Service Ribbon with one campaign star. The badge, a symbol of the front-line fighting man, distinguished the combat soldiers from rear area and service troops. It consists of a miniature replica of a Revolutionary War flint-lock rifle mounted on a blue background and superimposed on a wreath.

The *Daily News* mentioned the oddly named hills which came mostly from the imaginations of G.I.s and war correspondents. Some of the names included: Jane Russell Hill, Sniper Ridge, Christmas Hill, Pork Chop Hill, T-Bone Hill, Twin Peaks, Heartbreak Ridge, Punchbowl, Anchor Hill, and Jackson Heights…to name a few. None of the hills were found on regular maps, but the *Daily News* published an illustrated map, created by staff artist Krauss.

The Star-Ledger mentioned, in an article written by Lawrence Ragonese, more than 6000 Morris County Korean War veterans being honored, 50 years after the war, with special commemorative service medals that were approved by the county freeholders. The medals were ordered from an East Hanover firm, Achievement Products for $24,750. The front of the medal was designed by a committee of veterans. The county seal was encircled with the words "Morris County Distinguished Military Service." The back included an outline of the country map with the American flag with the words "Morris County Freeholders, Korean War Commemorative." It had a blue and white ribbon, the United Nation colors, since it was a U.N. military action. The ribbon was similar to the official Korean War Service Ribbon.

The ceremony was held on Tuesday, June 16, 2005 at the Morristown Armory, Morristown, New Jersey.

The New Jersey Distinguished Service Medal (DSM) is New Jersey's highest military award. It was originally issued in 1858 for distinguished service in the New Jersey Militia but was infrequently used until Governor Kean re-authorized it in 1988.

After the Spanish American War, the Mexican Border Expedition, and again, after World War I, the State of New Jersey minted special medals for returning New Jersey veterans to honor their service. After World War II, Korea, Vietnam, and subsequent combat actions, no such medal was authorized.

Governor Kean was seeking an appropriate way to honor returning combat veterans and acknowledge the debt the state owed them for their service, and therefore re-authorized the medal.

To be eligible for the medal, veterans had to meet the following criteria:

- A current resident of New Jersey.
- A resident of New Jersey at the time he entered into military service.
- Honorably discharged.
- Proof of serving in combat theater while on active duty during wartime.

Other military medals Domenic received included:

- Combat Infantryman Badge
- Good Conduct Medal
- National Defense Service Medal
- Korean Service Medal (with three bronze stars)
- United Nations Service Medal
- Army's Combat Infantryman Badge (CIB), which Domenic said was earned after the first encounter with the enemy.
- The State of New Jersey Senate & General Assembly Citation

Domenic is very humble about his awards. He said, "It's the ones that didn't come back that deserve the honor. They are the real heroes."

In recent years, restaurants such as Charlie Brown's Steakhouse and Applebee's, honored veterans and active duty military to have a free meal on Veteran's Day as a show of appreciation for bravery and service.

The Infantry Soldier

By Domenic Lombardi

I would like to dedicate this poem to all of our veterans of the Korean War, especially to my dear friends and buddies: Joseph Russo, David Lunasco, Frank Zachar, Dean Fultz, Jerry Pugh, James Lavey, Larry Day, Robert Malone, Raymond Clark, Robert Kammerer, Earl Avers, Ralph Bocuzo, Truman Turner, Robert Tarr, Roger Otterson, Homer Tomes, and Sergeant Wainwright.

Tall and short, lean and mean, young and old faces clean.

Rifles and packs slung on their backs; out in front the point man tracks.

Burp! Burp! Soldiers hit the ground, the enemy our column have found.

Five yards apart! Squads command: Move out! Move out! Our objective sought.

Oh! Infantry soldier, a battle to be fought. Climb and claw your way up the ridge.

For now, we have finally grossed that bridge, shells a bursting, rifle fire we must face.

Oh! Infantry I see them fall in their place, push on! Push on! Our objective sought.

The smoke has cleared a battle well-fought, our infantry he stands tall.

For he has done the job, he answered the call. My buddies were not as lucky and died.

For them I must admit I cried. Oh! Lord, accept my buddies into your fold.

Infantry and a soldier he did what told. Our hats off for a job well done.

To me, the infantry soldier is second to none.

Our Heroes

By Alexandra Lombardi (granddaughter) at the age of 8

O stands for obstacles. The obstacles our veterans have faced.

U stands for united. Our country is united because of you.

R stands for respect. The respect of all, you deserve.

H stands for honor. We honor you today.

E stands for effort. The effort you put forth is why we are free.

R stands for rights. The rights of free speech, free religion and the right to vote.

O stands for one. We are one nation under God.

E stands for each of you. The sacrifices each of you have made for us.

S stands for served. You have served your country well.

Chapter 36

By Domenic

Under the G.I. bill I thought that my job was secure when I was returned to civilian life. The company that I had worked for had not one Korea veteran return to work. I was the first to come home and return to my job. I didn't take any time in getting back to my job like some who would rather collect than go right back to work.

When I left the job, I was learning to operate a press. The company at the time wasn't union and if you were the boss's pet you received the best job and the most pay. Yeah, we had such individuals working in our department.

When I came back to work, the people were just in the process of starting a union. Knowing I didn't stand a chance with brownnosers, I became involved with the union as a representative we called Shop Stewards. I did not complain until we organized, and the shop was now union. To add to our forgotten warriors, I was up against a tyrant of a boss who hated unions, thus he disliked me now more than ever.

The seniority list was made out for the men in their various jobs in the department. Now my boss had two prima donnas he chose over me for the job I was supposed to have. I didn't say anything to him but went right into our personnel manager.

He tried to give me the runaround. He told me that I had been away for two years, thus I had lost two years seniority.

I didn't argue with him and I told him that I was going down to my draft board to see if he was right.

He quickly changed his tone and said, "Don't worry, I'll take care of it."

A week went by and I just happened to come across a memo on my boss's desk. It was the seniority list and sure enough he had his two cronies ahead of me on the list. He walked into the office and I confronted him with the list.

He got very belligerent with me and told me that he would not change the list.

Well, I guess Korea came out of me and I grabbed him by the collar and lifted him off the chair. I wanted to punch him out, but I knew it would foil my chances, so I dropped him down in his chair. I told him, "I'm going to the Veterans Administration because both you and the personnel director lied to me and stuck your own buddies in front of me."

Two days later I was called into the personnel director's office and he handed me the seniority list, and my name was where it was supposed to be—finally.

So, you see, we Korea veterans were scoffed at even by our own. All I ever heard was, "You guys had it made because it was just a 'police action.'"

I never discussed Korea ever again at work with anyone except my good buddy who was a World War II veteran. He helped me in my job and when he became foreman of the department, he made me his assistant foreman. That was the start of my career with the company that I worked for over 42 years and retired. But you can see that if you have an idiot in charge, he isn't good for the company—he is more less in a rut with his cronies.

What made me even more furious was that these two other individuals were supposed to be shown how to do my job. I said to the boss, "What do you think I am—an idiot? You teach them. You're the boss, aren't you?"

When a new supervisor, Bill Ferraro, took over we changed over to union rules for promotions and increases. The men were paid according to their ability to work and their skills—not by who they knew in the company.

From that day forward we were strictly union and most all the time things ran smoothly. But I realized I was at a dead-end job and the only way up was to get some more schooling. I enrolled in a night school for business management. I studied at night and completed the course in three years with some pretty decent grades. The results were sent to our personnel department and that opened the door for my first salaried position with the company.

I still thought that I needed some more smarts, so I enrolled in television and industrial electronics at RET's (Research Experience for Teachers) school in Kearny, New Jersey. I attended night classes twice a week. I took the course for one year and graduated.

For awhile I considered going into TV repair on my own, but my job was going along fine and my pay was increased every year with a bonus. So, I was thinking about getting moved up and enrolled in locksmith school. It was a one-year course, all hands on, with keys and locks to work on. With plenty of book work and lessons that had to be completed, I finished and got my certificate for a Class A locksmith license. Little did I know—our plant engineer would have a by-pass operation and would not return to the plant. I was asked to take over his job.

I thought my boss was crazy and told him, "No way. I am not qualified."

After a few days they called me into the general manager's office. He told me that he had enough confidence in my ability to run the plant wit all my years of working around the machinery. I took the job and I lasted about four or five years, then I was asked to take over the third shift. They were planning to expand the operation and needed someone with my experience to head the operation. What a snow job, for I did run the third shift a few years earlier and it just about killed me. My body clock would never adjust, and I would find myself sleeping at the dinner table while eating. Even when we had some company over before I would leave for work, we would be sitting around the table talking and I would fall asleep right in the chair. So, when they asked me to take that job, I refused and chose to take an early retirement. After 42 years with that company, I retired at 60-years-old. They gave me an excellent package: my salary requirement from the company; my union pension; and because I was not yet old enough to collect social security, they compensated me until I was old enough to collect at 62.

I saw so many changes in manufacturing over the years with this company—some good for the worker, some not. Automation, something I never thought would invade our industry did. And I saw our department drop from 60 employees to 30 in just one year. That wasn't the end of that either, for newer equipment was purchased and one machine did twice the work of the two put together.

Chapter 37

By Domenic

Antoinette and I were married on April 19, 1953 at Our Lady of the Valley Church, Orange, New Jersey. A reception followed at the White Eagle Auditorium, Bloomfield, New Jersey.

We had planned our own wedding and paid for all the festivities. Our parents had no involvement other than giving us their blessings. Usually a bride's father's family pays for the wedding of his daughter. In our situation, the bride's father thought differently and refused, so that left it up to me and Toni to pay for the wedding. So, with $800 or $900 we arranged the whole wedding from start to finish.

The weddings of our era were nothing compared to the weddings of today. In our day we usually rented a huge hall, purchased cold cuts, rolls, Italian cookies by the tray for each table, all flavors of soda, and usually an experienced uncle who could tap a keg of beer.

The night before the wedding we all gathered in the kitchen and began to assemble our sandwiches of ham and cheese, salami and cheese, and some baloney and cheese. It took many hours filling up the sandwiches and wrapping them and putting them in boxes for the trip to the hall we rented for our wedding.

We hustled up a band to play—a cousin had a small band. Our limo driver was a neighbor. Father Meckler officiated.

The reception was very informal. Seating was given out to the immediate family. After that it was sit with whoever you chose.

Our wedding was a customary "Football Wedding" because the sandwiches were with the bartender in a box. All you had to do was tell him the type you wanted, and he would pass it to you on the fly, hoping you could catch it. Today such a wedding is out of the question—if you don't spend thousands, how would you face your friends?

Despite all the work we had to do, everyone enjoyed the wedding broke, but thank God Toni had some money. That's how we were able to purchase our first home.

I applied for a G.I. loan at a whopping rate of 4.5 percent on a loan of $11,000. I had to get a part time job to qualify for the loan because I wasn't making enough at my present job as a dye cutter at the time. I started working in Uncle Joe's machine shop at night. Thank God that only lasted a few weeks, for I increased my salary at my day job and was lucky to be making $55 per week. The mortgage for the month was as mere $44—and that was still a struggle. Hard work and many hours—with some advancements and pay increases—made life become a little easier.

Then along came the County Road Commission. It was decided to condemn a group of homes and ours was in that group. Now we had lawyers fighting for a better deal than was offered by the county.

I don't know or remember how many times we had to appear in the courthouse in Newark. After months of fighting we all agreed to the conditions and the money.

Now we had the option to leave the house. Or if we agreed to stay, we were responsible to move the house off the land at our own expenses.

The next move was hitting contractors. We had a local contractor who had bid on the fives homes to be moved. Now we had to find a contractor who moved houses. When we found a contractor--who was capable of doing the job-- we were ready to sign the contracts. The county gave us a deadline and the work began as soon as we all signed our contract. Now, once the house was in the process of being lifted and moved, we had to vacate the house and moved in with Toni's mom and dad for nine weeks—the time it took them to get the house back onto the new foundation.

In order for us to get approval to move the houses back, we had to purchase a similar lot in the rear of our property. This we had to buy from a man who owned all the property behind our homes at the time. The property was all wooded and it was necessary to have all the trees chopped down before they could work on the foundation. I got a sharp ax and chopped down all the trees on that 50-foot x 100-foot strip of land. The bulldozer operator told me that he would take care of the stumps with the machine. So, every day I came home from work and went out and chopped trees until they were all down.

Every day I made my usual trip up after work to check on the contractors. All went well until, on one visit, I saw the surveyors' stakes set for the foundation to be dug for my house. I measured the distance from the neighbor's driveway and saw it was close to his property. So, I pulled the stakes out.

The contract saw the stakes missing and called me. "Who pulled the stakes?"

"I did. And I want the stakes moved over so our house will be in the center of my lot," I said.

He wasn't too happy, but he did what I asked.

A week or two later, on my visit to check on the plumbers I walked into the basement. They were hooking up an old water tank. I asked them, "Do you know what you're doing? Stop right where you are. I paid for a new hot water heater to be installed…not that antique. I want the *new* water heater."

I went directly to the contractor's home and told him the guys were installing that old water tank. I said, "I think you should get over there and watch the job to make sure this will not happen again.

Then came the day they were finished with all the foundation and the next day they would drop the house down onto the new foundation. I walked down into the basement and some of the men had just finished some work around the chimney. I looked at the chimney and said to the mason, "Isn't that built a little too high for the amount of drop between the present chimney and what you guys put up?"

You guessed it! They quickly removed a layer of bricks. Had they left it when the house was lowered the next day, the chimney would have pushed up through the house and roof.

Watching every move proved to be a money saver in accidents and helpful in getting the job done. Before we signed the contract to move the house back, we decided that we would need some extra room for the kids. We had the contractor add to the back of the house a 14-foot by 20-foot addition. He would erect the shell and I would finish the inside. I had ordered all the material needed and each day I came home from work, we worked on the rooms until 11 p.m.

Being a rather small addition, I divide the room, making one large and the other small. I carried all the sheetrock from the garage into the house myself. I installed all the insulation and ran all the electric outlets. And Toni helped with the sheetrock. I had asked for help only one time and that was because the sheetrock was 14 footers and no way could I do it alone or even with the help of Toni.

I asked Joe and Peter Schrilla to help with the ceilings. Once up, I did all the rest of the sheetrock for both rooms. I did all the taping and spackling for the rooms. I built a closet in the large room and a small one in the smaller room. I installed all the trim and finished the windows.

Next, I had to install the flooring for each room. We went to purchase our tile and the floor was installed. I installed two new doors for the bedrooms and completed the electrical outlets and the fixtures for both rooms. While all this was taking place so was the task of fixing the outside. The driveway was nothing but mud and dirt. Luckily, I had my brother-in-law who worked for P.S. Gas. Whenever he had a load of gravel at the end of his shift, he would come and dump it in my driveway. I would spread the gravel as he dumped it until we had all that I needed. Next, he would call me and tell me he would be dumping a load of asphalt he had left from his job. He dumped and I would rake it out. I used a garden roller to roll it out smooth. After a few weeks of this I had almost a complete finished driveway—no mud.

Once we had most of the inside done, we now had to grade the outside. Many loads of dirt were dropped by our contractor and spread over the front and back yards. Next, grass seed was spread, and bushes and trees were planted. I built a retaining wall in the driveway in front of the house to hold my lawn in check.

The backyard required much more work because it was considerably lower than our neighbor's property. This meant much more dirt to be dumped and spread.

In order to move the garage, the contractor had to build a foundation –and in addition to that three rows of cinder block to bring the level of the garage in line with the driveway. Before we could move the garage, I had to get an order from the county for permission to fill a mosquito ditch that ran through our properties. Their first suggestion was a bridge across the ditch into my garage.

I told them, "No way. I have small children and I don't want a bridge." We got permission but had to sign a waiver of some kind to protect ourselves against a lawsuit.

With the rooms completed, now came the job of painting them.

The rest of our days were spent getting the yard in shape. The garage needed a new roof and that was my next weekend project.

After a few years we seemed to catch up on all our repairs around the house. One evening I decided to convert our front porch into a closed-in entrance way. It had windows all around and I wanted it more private and with more room for entering the front. The kids were growing up and we needed a place for them to entertain their friends. We decided to finish the basement.

I had a buddy who worked for Two Guys in Totowa, New Jersey. I explained to him what I planned to do, and he told me to come to Two Guys and he would give me a break on the materials needed. I went one night after work and he loaded my station with 2x4s, boxes of ceiling tiles, and paneling. My wagon was so loaded I couldn't fit some boxes. We met another buddy and he agreed to take the extra boxes for me in his car.

I framed the cellar walls and partitioned the furnace room and the bathroom from the main room. I installed the electric outlets and the ceiling fixtures and the wall switches. Then I installed the ceiling tiles for the whole basement except the furnace room.

To use the basement during the colder months we needed some heat. I went to Sears and picked up a gas fired wall furnace. I hooked the gas, electric, and the flue for the new heater.

Since we entertained often, it was necessary to have a sink installed. We got a sink from Antonio who had just installed a new one in his kitchen and gave us his old one.

Well, the basement worked out very well and we did have many parties. Outside during the hot summer days, we figured why not get an above-ground pool for the kids? We had ordered one and the guys came to erect the pool and a small deck to accompany the pool. This kept the kids pretty busy during the summer months while school was out. But what good is a pool if you don't have a patio?

Toni rounded up some nice slates and I laid the foundation for a patio floor next to our garage. That was okay for a day or two, but when it rained, we had to run in the house. So now I purchased some 2x4s from Channel and some long plastic panels for the roof. We had found some large screens and they fit the bill for walls of the patio. I installed some light fixtures and switches for the patio.

To keep the pool area safe for any kids wandering around, I carted wood from my job every day until I had enough for a fence around the whole pool. The hard part was not erecting the fence but painting it. The fence only lasted about five years before showing signs of rot. Someone that our son Domenic knew threw away a chain link fence and he dropped it off in our yard. I removed the old wooden fence and installed the new chain link fence around the pool. I had two gates for the pool entrance. This fence was much better, and it was safe for any kids that might wander into the pool area.

After Toni's mother passed, her father, Gabrielle, had come to live with us, which made it very difficult, for we had only three bedrooms. He originally lived with Toni's sister, Connie, but she passed of cancer.

We looked for another house—without much luck. We wanted to find an area where her dad could get involved in activities. We got tired of looking and decided to expand our present house. We contacted a builder and together we worked out a plan for an addition. We ended up installing two bedrooms and a full bath up on the second floor. Everything was progressing along just fine.

Once the roof was installed on the new addition, the men installed the plywood sheeting. I left for work on morning and the men would be installing the shingles. I expected to see the whole new addition done with shingles when I came home that night from work. I pulled into the driveway and walked to the rear of my house and saw the guys removing the shingles. "What in the world are you guys doing?" I asked.

Our township inspector had them remove the shingles because of a new code. The plywood-sheeting they installed was a new brand and the code requirement for it was that between each sheet installed you must maintain a quarter inch spacing for expansion. I told the contractor, "Those shingles you put back better be new...and not the old ones you took off."

We had to wait for the township inspector to come and give them an "okay" to continue.

Well, I waited for that inspector to come and when he came, I told him a few things he didn't want to hear: "Get your butt in and inspect the job! And I don't want to see you come back for any more mistakes you may have caused me."

The addition was completed by the contractor and we did all the interior decorating. With two bedrooms and a full bath, we now had sufficient room for Antoinette's father, with plenty of sleeping room for all. We even utilized a small attic space for storing of clothes and a den for Toni and me to watch television in private.

We also had purchased a large refrigerator with an ice hook up. It was so large that I had to tear down part o the kitchen wall to get it into the kitchen, which ultimately gave us another large archway into the dining area from the kitchen. We did get our kitchen redone with all new cabinets, a new stove and a new dishwasher. We had someone install the flooring and the job was complete. In the place where our old stove once stood, we had the contractor build us a little breakfast nook for two. The kitchen was small for a large group, so we used our dining room for larger groups.

You can sum up to over 40 years in this house as one big experience. How many people do you know that have to move? And I don't mean moving out to another location. I mean moving your whole house to another location! Starting out with a one-story, two-bedroom, and adding on two more. Then years later, adding an upper floor with two bedrooms and another full bath.

Had this house satisfied our needs over the years? I would have to say "yes." For a mere investment of $11,500, plus $25,000 and some over the span of 44 years, the day we moved the selling price of the house was $197,000, plus an interest no bank could ever equal on a $33,000 considering we lived and enjoyed every day in the house.

It was rather strange that our house number at first was 44 Beaufort Ave. and our G.I. mortgage was $44 a month and we moved out of the house after 44 years.

Why did we move? For more than one reason. The first was most of our old neighbors either moved or passed away. Across the street from us the land was being purchased for a shopping center, thus all our neighbors across the road would be leaving. The second reason was Mr. Lam, the owner of Lam's Restaurant on the circle, was purchasing most of the houses along our strip. Ours being one of the last, he would have to gain control. Third, the ones that he did buy were on either side of our house and the tenants he had in them were not desirable people. They abused the houses and the property. And they were not friendly. So, it was a godsend that he finally gave us a reasonable offer. We thought, *Let's get out of here before we are the last and he will have the best bargaining power.*

That is why we had to make the decision to leave 284 Eisenhower Parkway, Livingston, N.J. We lived in the same house but moved the house and 44 Beaufort Ave. because 284 Eisenhower Parkway.

Chapter 38

By Antoinette

Sixty-two years, five children, 13 grandchildren, and five great-grandchildren later—Domenic and I are still in love.

Our five children and their children are:

Domenic and his wife Deborah. Their children are Donna Marie (and her husband Arthur), and David (and his wife Courtney). Donna Marie and Arthur have three children: Scarlett Rose, Liliana, and Brielle.

Diane and her husband Antonio. Their children are Sal (and his wife Yesenia), Domenic (and his wife Anna), and Caterina. Caterina and her husband Bryan have a son named Bryan. Domenic and Anna have a daughter named Diane.

Mary Anne and her late husband Anthony. Their children are Anthony (and his fiancée Melissa), Marianna, Antoinette, Andrea, and Domenic. Kathleen and her husband Raymond. Gary and his wife Amy. Their children are Alexandra, Domenic, and Gary.

At Domenic's 80th birthday celebration, we shared our love and joy with our family and friends—as well as Domenic's comrades in arms, including his corporal buddies Vincent Cerrato and John "Jack" Dalton of Florham Park and Sergeant Ralph Bocuzzo of Stamford, Connecticut.

I spent two months planning the party, which was held at Hanover Manor in East Hanover, New Jersey. More than 80 people attended.

The weather was terrible—drizzling and muggy. I didn't know if anyone would come. But it turned out great.

I presented pocket watches to Domenic's fellow veterans, including Robert Malone and Raymond Clark, who couldn't attend. We were all so close.

During the party Domenic read a written statement about his life, his military service, and most important, our love.

Today we are living next door to our daughter Mary Anne Ardolino. Mary Anne's husband died at the age of 42, leaving her with five children. We helped raise them.

We keep active by bowling, going to the movies, and playing Rummikub at the senior center. Dom plays cards. We also joined the 32nd Infantry Regiment, a veteran's organization founded by Chester and Janet Bair.

Janet Bair was a wonderful woman. She always asked Dom to write about Korea in their newsletter. He wrote so many articles. Chester passed away a long time ago and she did a good job taking over the organization.

In Celebration of Domenic's 80th Birthday

To Dad, from Gary

You may have thought I didn't see,

Or that I hadn't heard,

Life lessons that you taught to me,

But I got every word.

Perhaps you thought I missed it all,

And that we'd grow apart,

But, Dad, I picked up everything,

It's written on my heart.

Without you, Dad, I wouldn't be

The man I am today,

You built a strong foundation,

No one can take away.

I've grown up with your values,

And I'm very glad I did,

So Happy 80th birthday, Father,

From your forever grateful kid.

From friend, the late Marion Boscaino

Dom's 80ᵗʰ Birthday

We're all here tonight to celebrate Domenic's 80ᵗʰ birthday. So, let us raise our glass to Dom, who has a lot of class. A prince of a guy, yessiree! Though he can't fly as high as the young critters fly. He remains a true blue S.O.B. (Sweet Ole Buzzard).

If you ask Toni what it's like being married to Dom, she'll reply, "I named my first ulcer after him."

Dom's a committed Korean War Veteran, whose motto is "Never again." After 55 years of marriage, Toni's motto is also, "Never again."

Dom and Toni surprise we seniors weekly with their unison costumes for every occasion. They have more costumes than Bill Clinton has girlfriends.

Dom's job during the war was kitchen duty. He learned some valuable lessons such as "Big potatoes are easier to peel than small potatoes."

Dom and Toni met at a dance in Orange at the age of 13. They married 55 years ago and were blessed with five children and 13 grandchildren. In 1997 they moved to Florham Park. When Toni displayed her Easter Bunny collection on the front lawn, the neighbors thought Hugh Hefner moved his N.Y. Bunny Club to Florham Park.

The couple exercise daily. Dom believes "a word to the WIDE" is sufficient. And exercise has its merits. The ole boy looks great. His suits fit like a glove. Too bad they don't fit like suits.

Dom was never tempted by "Wine, Women, and Song." The delivery boy from the local liquor store thought Dom was having an affair since he overhead him saying, "I'm going home with a cold duck."

For Toni's birthday, Dom gave her a beautiful looking glass, to which Toni asks, "Mirror, mirror, on the wall, who's the biggest pain in the butt of all?" Dom thinks that she is, but we all know that it is he.

In conclusion, we all love you dearly. There's an old adage that says, "We only tease the people we love."

Again, Happy 80th birthday. And may God grant us many more celebrations together.

Words from granddaughter, Andrea Ardolino, age 19

Living next door to my grandparents, they were always good role models to me. I always tell them that it's amazing they could be together that long.

Grandpa risked his life in war. He jokes around and is fun to be with. He gives me good advice about school, work, and studying. I'm in County College in Morris, working my way toward a nursing program.

Grandma would do anything for anyone. She's a good person. And really energetic for her age. She makes holidays fun for the family with games. The food is good. Her meatballs and her chicken cutlets are my favorite dishes.

It was fun when I was a little girl. They had a cat I was close with. We all watched TV together. Sometimes I slept over and they made pancakes in the morning.

On Grandpa's 80th birthday, I was only 13. I don't remember much of the speech he made, but he mentioned that I was his guardian angel. I thought that was really nice.

Their house is still like my second home. I'm there constantly.

Poetry from Domenic, to Antoinette, while in service

"Be My Love"

Be my love—

for no one else can

end this yearning

This need that you and

you alone create

Just the way you fill my arms

the way you fill my dreams

The dreams that you inspire

With every sweet desire

Be my love

And with your kisses set me

burning

One kiss is all I need to seal

my faith

And hand in hand

We'll find love's promised land

There'll be no one but you for me

eternally

If you will be my love

I do believe that God above,

Created you for me to love.

He picked you out from all the rest,

Because he knew I'd love you best.

I once had a heart both brave and true,

But now it's gone from me to you.

Take care of it as I have done,

For you have two and I have none.

If when I get to heaven and you're not there,

I'll paint your face on a golden stair.

And if you don't come by Judgement Day,

I'll know you're gone the other way.

I'll give the angels back their wings,

Their golden halos and all those things.

And just to prove my love for you,

I'll go to hell dear just for YOU!

Poetry from Antoinette, to Domenic, during his time in service

"Because of You"

Because of you there's a song in my heart

Because of you my romance had a start

Because of you the sun will shine, the moon and the stars will say you're mine forever and ever to part

I only live for your love and your kiss

It's paradise to be near you like this

Because of you my life is now worthwhile, and I can smile

Because of YOU!

I wake up each morning and hum a tune

'Cause you will be home way before June

It is then you know I'll be 23

And hope this is my last year to be FREE!

I'm sitting by the window, thinking of you, My Darling, wherever you are.

Because there's no tomorrow, you are always in my heart.

It's a sure thing I love you, Baby, won't you say you love me.

Where are you, Harold of my Heart?

You're my desire.

You're so understanding.

Beautiful hazel eyes.

Night and day, I'll always love you.

Lover come back to me.

Are you lonesome tonight Lover?

Maybe I'll be seeing you, again, by the light of the silvery moon.

Goodnight, sweetheart, goodnight.

"Our Hearts Must Wait"

I know your heart is lonely and you know that mine is too,

But what's there, this side of earth that you or I can do.

I cannot walk across the sea or over pass the land,

To see your loving smile again,

To hold your gentle hand.

I cannot turn the clock ahead to bring the hour near,

And I have not the magic wand to make the weather clear.

And, so, we have to save our dreams while we are apart,

And live in silent message that warm the waiting heart.

But there will be a morning, when, the shore will anchor ships,

And then your charms will fill my arms and I shall kiss your lips.

I can't live without you,

And you can't live without me.

So, let's not forget each other,

But love and cherish each other,

For the rest of our life.

I met a wonderful guy,

At the age of 14.

I call him "Stinky."

And he calls me "Porky."

Now he's Porky and I am Stinky.

Ha-ha.

Though many the changes,

This past year has brought,

Let's keep it together,

In memory and thought.

And make it a future of love worthwhile.

It is hard to find the words to express

All the love and laughter

That you have brought me

I hope our love for each other

Will never die.

If all our wishes were to come true,

We'd have a little bungalow just meant for two.

A year would pass and then perhaps,

We'd add some rooms for a couple of tots.

D—stands for Darling

O—"Oh" how I miss you

M—Miles, how far away you are

E—stands for empty, the way my heart is now

N—nearness, hope it will be soon

I—Incomplete

C—Careful, be on the alert my love.

Roses are red

Violets are blue

Sugar is sweet

But who cares,

Because we have each other

To love the rest of our life.

No matter where life leads us,

Whether we're far away or near,

I'll always be thinking of you,

My love who is very dear.

No matter how many lovers have to struggle through life,

They must keep up their chin and fight.

And never give up,

Because when two people love each other deeply,

Love can never die.

And neither can we.

I have a lover both brave and true,

Who's fighting right now for the red, white, and blue.

I miss him; I love him and someday real soon,

He'll come back to me with arms wide open,

And we'll smooch under the moon.

Somehow, I still can't believe,

We two are so far apart,

But someday soon you'll all return,

And that's when we'll make a new start.

I shall begin this little poem,

By saying, "Hurry home!"

I've got the pots and pans and stuff,

So, soldier, hurry, and phone!

There's not more room left in the house,

For silverware and such,

So, when we are ready to say, "I do,"

My mother will thank you so much.

Whenever I think of you,

I think of the things we used to do,

The rides in the country,

Our trips to the shore,

Going to the auction,

All seemed like such a bore.

Yet now I know I would enjoy,

Most anything like that,

To have you near I'd even adore,

Just sitting chewing the fat.

Just sitting here thinking that March is here,

And, somehow, I feel that you are near.

For now, I know counting days will be fun,

And soon I'll hear you calling me "Hun."

Christmas came and Christmas went,

And, as usual, Santa was a gent.

He left me sweaters, slips, and such,

And how I wonder did I deserve so much.

Porky and Stinky are sweethearts,

Until Uncle Sam said, "Come on."

Porky and Stinky are letter sweethearts now,

Until Stinky comes home with a Wow!

Got your letter and boy, oh boy,

Couldn't tell you of all my joy.

I read "two weeks more" over and over,

'Cause this letter was sure my four-leaf clover.

God made so many wonderful things,

The flowers, the trees, and the birds that sing.

Yet best of all he created you.

Then made me,

And gave us our cue.

I feel a bit proud these few months you're away,

Perhaps it's just that I've begun to pray.

For never before had I wanted so much,

To extend my hand and feel your touch.

Final thoughts from Maryanne Christiano-Mistretta, editor of this book

Helping Domenic and Antoinette Lombardi prepare their book for publication was delightful. I enjoyed their company every step of the way and was teary-eyed as we came to a close because I knew, in my heart, I'd miss them dearly.

But Antoinette told me, "We'll stay friends and keep in touch. You're always welcome to come over."

This beautiful couple stole my heart! Domenic and Antoinette are obviously still very much in love. They are so much fun and were always cracking jokes—often at the other's expense.

When I worked in their home, I was not treated as just an editor. I was treated like FAMILY.

I am honored and humbled to have worked with Domenic and Antoinette. The experience was a blessing from God.

(Top left to right) Antoinette, Domenic (Bottom) Wedding Day

(Top Left) Palmer, (Middle) Antoinette & Domenic, (Right) Domenic, (Bottom Row) Antoinette & Domenic

(Top) Antoinette & Domenic, (Bottom) Gary, Kathleen, Mary Ann, Diane & Domenic

Special Thanks...

Thanks to the New Jersey Korean War Veterans Memorial Commission—Domenic and Antoinette Lombardi

Thanks to Maryanne for her time and effort in getting my story in writing. I will be forever grateful—Domenic Lombardi

To Mrs. Olga Petrilak—I want to thank Olga for introducing us to Maryanne—Antoinette Lombardi

And most of all, to our family for your love and support, including our late, beloved cats, Rocky and Bullet— Domenic and Antoinette

Other titles from Higher Ground Books & Media:

Wise Up to Rise Up by Rebecca Benston

A Path to Shalom by Steen Burke

Overcomer by Forrest Henslee

Miracles: I Love Them by Forest Godin

Out of Darkness by Stephen Bowman

Dear You by Derra Nicole Sabo

I Don't Want to Be Like You by Maryanne Christiano-Mistretta

Shameless Persistence by Sandra Bretting

Jack Kramer's Journey by Frank Adkins

Chronicles of a Spiritual Journey by Stephen Shepherd

The Real Prison Diaries by Judy Frisby

Add these titles to your collection today!

http://www.highergroundbooksandmedia.com

Do you have a story to tell?

Higher Ground Books & Media is an independent Christian-based publisher specializing in stories of triumph! Our purpose is to empower, inspire, and educate through the sharing of personal experiences.

Please visit our website for our submission guidelines.

http://www.highergroundbooksandmedia.com

www.ingramcontent.com/pod-product-compliance
Lightning Source LLC
LaVergne TN
LVHW011348080426
835511LV00005B/182